The Deployed Data Scientist

MLOps and Analytics in Practice

Ankit Anand
Scott Burk
Kinshuk Dutta

Technics Publications
SEDONA, ARIZONA

TECHNICS PUBLICATIONS

115 Linda Vista, Sedona, AZ 86336 USA
https://www.TechnicsPub.com

Edited by Steve Hoberman
Cover design by Lorena Molinari

First Printing 2026

ISBN, print ed. 9798898160982
ISBN, Kindle ed. 9798898160999
ISBN, PDF ed. 9798898161002

Library of Congress Control Number: 2026940426

Ankit's dedication:

To my parents Dr Anil Kant Mishra and Usha Mishra, who show me the path ahead each day.
To my wife, Sakshi, and daughters, Anshika and Aishani, who give me the reason to follow the path every day!

Scott's dedication:

To my wife Jackie, thank you for all your support and for the greatest adventure of my life. You are simply the best.

Kinshuk's dedication:

To my parents, Krishna Dutta and Lal Mohan Dutta, for teaching me that strong foundations make lasting work possible.
To my wife, Noirita, and daughter, Rachael, for reminding me that even in production, life's most important systems are built on love, patience, and purpose.

Acknowledgments

This book reflects the support and encouragement of many people, to whom I owe my deepest thanks.

Special Thanks to a few of my colleagues and friends who have always helped me in both professional and personal life - Dennis, Kinshuk, Neel, Ashley, and Upendra. Thank you for all the possible ways you have helped me out!

I offer my humble thanks for all the blessings from Dadajee, Dadi Ma, Nanajee, and Nani Ma. To my family: my loving Mom Usha Mishra and Dad Dr. Anil Kant Mishra, and my dear Mother-in-law Anita Jha and Father-in-law Awadhesh Kumar Jha, your unwavering belief has been my foundation. To my brother, Anshuman Ankur, and my sister-in-law, Puja, thank you for your constant support. To my brother-in-law, Ankesh, for always being around to listen to me.

To all my uncles, aunts, and cousins, thank you for your continued support and love.

To my incredible wife, Sakshi, your patience, love, and partnership made this possible. And to my wonderful children – Anshika, Aishani, Aanvi, and Avyansh – you are my greatest joy and inspiration. My heartfelt gratitude extends to every member of my entire family for your enduring encouragement.

A special thank you to Mr. Vinoth Edwards, my teacher, mentor, and friend, for your invaluable guidance.

To my friends, Clement, Jesse, Ankur, and Amit, thank you for the enriching conversations and camaraderie.

Finally, my sincere respect and gratitude to all my current and former colleagues. I have learned immensely from each of you on this professional journey.

Ankit Anand

Contents

Introduction

This book provides a comprehensive, practitioner-focused guide to the discipline of Machine Learning Operations (MLOps), navigating the critical shift from experimental data science to the deployment of reliable, production-grade data products. The most significant challenges in machine learning are not algorithmic but operational. The book directly addresses the common "silent failures" and "it works on my machine" problems that plague data teams by establishing a robust, engineering-driven framework.

The core thesis is a fundamental mindset shift: treating data models not as one-off "projects," but as durable, auditable, and reliable "data products." The text systematically covers the end-to-end MLOps lifecycle, beginning with a foundational data strategy that includes the modern data stack, data governance, and the critical concept of Data Contracts.

The central part of the book builds out the "automated assembly line" for data products, providing deep dives into Model Engineering, automated CI/CD Pipelines, scalable Cloud Infrastructure, and advanced Model Monitoring and Observability. These chapters provide the complete technical blueprint for building, deploying, and managing models with confidence.

Finally, the book explores the frontiers of modern deployment. It covers advanced patterns like Explainable AI (XAI) and Human-in-the-Loop (HITL) frameworks, as well as a comprehensive guide to the new discipline of LLMOps for Generative AI, including RAG architectures and hallucination monitoring. The book concludes with a strategic playbook for data leaders to navigate the vendor landscape, structure high-performing teams, and manage the economics of AI.

Chapter 1

The Mindset Shift

We never set out to become "data people." If anyone had asked us fifteen to twenty years ago, we would not have even known what the term meant. As developers, our world was the Java Virtual Machine or a compiler; our professional lives revolved around a set of comforting, predictable principles. We thought in terms of design patterns, SOLID principles, and the elegant certainty of object-oriented programming. It was a world of logic where the compiler was our brutally honest friend. It told us exactly when and where we had made a mistake. There was no ambiguity. It compiled, or it didn't. Life, for the most part, was simple.

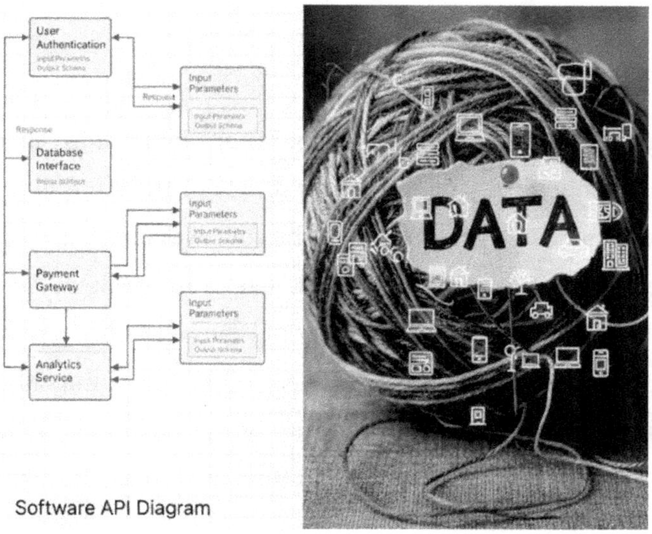

Figure 1.1. The two worlds: the comforting structure of code versus the beautiful chaos of real-world data.

Then, one afternoon, we were handed what was described as a "minor analytics task." An innocent-sounding request, wasn't it? A quick analysis for a major telecom client whose billing system (one we had built) had spat out a wildly inaccurate invoice. The system itself was working perfectly, no exceptions thrown, no errors in the logs. The logic was sound. But the output was nonsensical. The problem wasn't in the code; it was somewhere in the murky depths of the data it was processing.

That "small task" turned out to be the on-ramp to a career that dragged us, sometimes kicking and screaming, away from the clean room of software engineering and into the messy, unpredictable world of data. This journey led us through Master Data Management (MDM), enterprise architecture, machine learning, and eventually to the design of the very systems this book is about.

Field Story: The Ghost in the Join

Every data professional has a war story. A tale of a bug so insidious, so baffling, that it makes you question your career choices, the nature of reality, and how much caffeine a human body can safely absorb. This is ours.

The Setup: A Flawless Plan

The project was a big one: migrate customer billing history into a shiny new data warehouse. The prize at the end of this rainbow? A single, glorious source of truth for all financial reporting. Our team of developers had built an elegant pipeline. The code was clean, the logic was sound, and the test runs were perfect. Our team was confident. We were brilliant. We were, in hindsight, dangerously naive. The source system was a crusty old monolith, but it was the trusted system of record. It dutifully spat out a massive CSV file every night containing all the day's transactions: customer name, transaction date, amount, and the holy grail of relational data: the customer ID. The job was simple: ingest, join, and profit (metaphorically, of course). We were ready for a smooth, textbook deployment.

The Nightmare Begins

We went live at the end of the quarter. The "first" month-end reconciliation report ran overnight. In the morning, our customer's team opened the output, and it was pure, unadulterated chaos. It looked less like a financial report and more like a surrealist art exhibit. The grand totals were off by millions of dollars, which is generally frowned upon by the finance department. But the details were even more insane. One of the biggest, most loyal enterprise clients - a global behemoth - was apparently now in the business of buying a single $15 USB cable.

Meanwhile, a two-person startup they'd onboarded last week had, according to the flawless report, been a secret multi-million-dollar account for the past five years. The business stakeholders were, to put it mildly, not pleased. The pressure was on. The clock was ticking on the quarterly close. And the beautiful pipeline was producing fiction.

The Sleepless Night of Debugging

We immediately convened in a war room, armed with enough coffee and energy drinks to power a small city. What followed was a classic descent into developer madness.

Phase 1 (Hours 1-4): It's their Fault. Naturally, it was assumed we were the idiots. For the first four hours, it was a festival of frantic self-doubt.

- "Did you check the LEFT JOIN? Maybe it should be an INNER JOIN!"
- "Is it a CAST issue? Are they sure the IDs aren't being read as floats?"
- "Wait, could it be a weird character encoding problem from that one weird legacy system?"

We tore apart every line of our own SQL and Python code. We questioned our ability to write a simple SELECT statement. We found nothing. Our code was perfect. Annoyingly so.

Phase 2 (Hours 5-8): It's the Machine's Fault. Having exonerated ourselves, we moved on to blaming the infrastructure.

- "The ETL job log is green, but can we really trust the logs?"

- "Maybe the file got corrupted during the SFTP transfer! A single dropped bit!"
- "I'm telling you, it's a memory leak in the parser."

We were one step away from blaming solar flares and cosmic rays. Again, we found nothing. The file was intact. The pipeline ran successfully.

Phase 3 (Hours 9-12): Existential Despair. By 3 AM, the coffee had turned on us. The war room smelled of desperation and stale pizza. We were out of theories. We had proven that our code was correct, and the system had run it correctly. The only logical conclusion was that reality itself was flawed. We were ready to accept that the universe was fundamentally chaotic, and financial reconciliation was a lie.

The Dawn of Realization

The breakthrough didn't come from a brilliant insight. It came from giving up. We stopped looking at the whole broken system and decided to look at one. single. thing. We picked that invoice for "Global Corp Inc." The data showed the invoice was tied to customer ID 1138115. We knew in the master table that "Global Corp Inc." was customer ID 8675309. This was the whole problem, right? The IDs were mismatched. So, we opened the multi-gigabyte source CSV file, the one we were sent, and searched for the transaction. We found it. The row contained the correct transaction details for the USB cable. The customer's name column in that row clearly said "Global Corp Inc." The customer ID column in that same row said 1138115. The silence in the room was deafening. The file itself was the source of the lie. The name and the ID were mismatched before the data ever touched our system. We called the emergency contact for the source system team. A very tired developer on their end logged into their database and looked up ID 1138115. It belonged to "Bob's Pretty Good Widgets Inc." A flaw in their export query was creating a demonic chimera of a dataset; it was taking the customer's name from one row and the ID from another. Our pipeline was just faithfully and accurately processing beautifully formatted garbage.

The Hard-Won Lessons

That sleepless night was a brutal but effective teacher. We now have three laws, forged in the fires of 4 AM debugging sessions.

- **Trust is for Family and Dogs, Not Data Feeds.** Never assume the data received is correct, even if it comes from a trusted internal system. Treat all incoming data as hostile.

- **Build an Immune System for Your Pipeline.** Your pipeline is no longer a passive pipe. It's now an active guard. It runs a small sample of records through a validation check against the source system's API. If it finds a mismatch between name and ID, it doesn't just fail; it screams. The pipeline now acts like a bouncer at the door of your database.

- **Data Contracts are Cheaper than Therapy.** The root of all this pain was a communication gap. We had no formal agreement with the source team defining what they would provide. Establishing a clear "data contract" that outlines schemas, keys, and validation rules is the first thing you do. It's less painful than explaining to your VP of Finance why his report is a work of fiction.

Case Study: The Silent Model Failure

Every data professional has a story about the model that broke their heart. It's the one that worked perfectly in the lab but failed spectacularly in the wild. It's a rite of passage, a humbling lesson that teaches you more than any textbook ever could. For someone, it might have come early in their journey into machine learning, and the scar tissue remains a valuable teacher to this day.

The Project: Predicting Customer Churn

The project was a classic business problem: predicting customer churn for a major telecommunications client. Our team had a rich dataset on user behavior, demographics, and transaction history. We were excited. This was a chance to demonstrate the power of predictive analytics at scale.

We poured everything into it. We conducted rigorous exploratory data analysis, engineered dozens of clever features, and benchmarked several algorithms. After meticulous hyperparameter tuning, our Gradient Boosting model achieved something remarkable: 94% accuracy on our held-out test set. The number made everyone in the boardroom sit up straight.

The Deployment and Initial Success

We had followed the playbook to the letter. We received a static CSV file, a clean snapshot of the world. We documented our work in beautifully organized Jupyter notebooks and created a slide deck filled with elegant visualizations: ROC curves, feature importance plots, and precision-recall curves. The presentation was a triumph. The project was greenlit for immediate deployment, and our work was marked "done." We were heroes.

For the first two weeks, everything seemed perfect. The model was running smoothly in production, and we received positive feedback from the business team.

The Unraveling

Then, the support tickets started trickling in. At first, they were isolated complaints. But within days, the trickle became a flood. The customer service team's reports were baffling. Customers flagged by our model as "high churn risk" and subsequently targeted with aggressive retention offers were, in fact, some of our clients' most loyal advocates. We were confused, and in some cases, angry about the unwanted attention.

Meanwhile, analytics revealed a wave of unexpected cancellations from customers that their model had confidently labeled as "safe." The model wasn't just wrong; it was poisonously, confidently wrong. It was actively costing the business money and eroding customer trust.

The Forensic Investigation

The panic set in. Our manager was getting hammered in executive meetings. The team assembled in a war room, frantically trying to diagnose the problem. Our first instinct was to re-run the original notebooks. Everything worked perfectly. No errors. The code was fine. The model architecture was sound. We loaded the pickled model file and ran it against the test set again, achieving 94% accuracy. The local environment was pristine.

The breakthrough came when a junior data analyst decided to manually inspect the raw data being fed into the live prediction script. She compared it column by column to the original training data. The culprit was insidious.

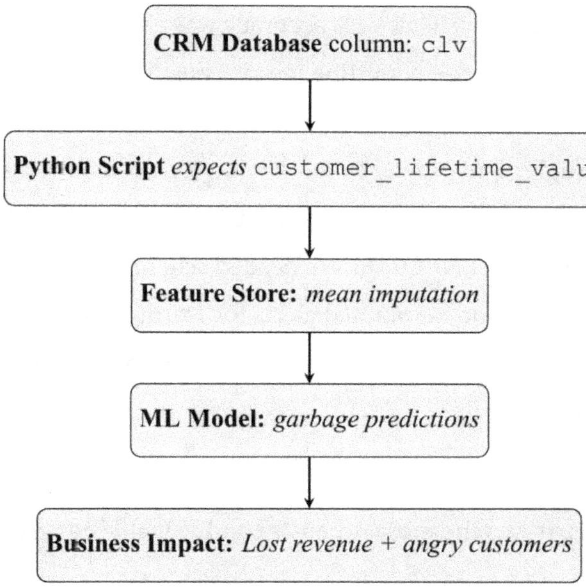

Figure 1.2. The cascade failure: How a simple column rename led to business impact.

The Root Cause

An upstream team in a completely different department, responsible for the customer relationship management database, made a minor schema change during a routine update. They had renamed a single column: "customer lifetime value" became clv. Our data ingestion pipeline, a series of Python scripts running on a cron schedule, didn't crash. It was written to be "robust," so if an expected column was missing, it would simply fill it with a null value rather than failing. And our model, cleverly designed to handle missing data, encountered these nulls and diligently imputed the mean from the training data for each customer. Every. Single. One. The model was making predictions based on a critical feature that had become meaningless garbage. It was flying blind but projecting total confidence.

Lessons Learned

We called it the "silent failure." It crystallized several truths that have defined many of our careers:

- **Models Don't Fail; Systems Do:** The algorithm was sound, but the system around it was fragile. We had treated the model as the final product, but the product was the entire system.
- **Accuracy is a Vanity Metric:** That 94% accuracy was a dangerous illusion that closed our eyes to the fragility of our system. Offline metrics mean nothing if the production data pipeline breaks.
- **Production is a Jungle:** The Jupyter notebook is a sterile lab. Production is a chaotic, interconnected ecosystem that changes unpredictably.
- **Validate Everything, Trust Nothing:** We needed schema validation tests, data distribution monitoring, and automated alerts for feature drift.
- **Own the Entire Pipeline:** Data scientists must take responsibility for the end-to-end system, not just the model itself.

This experience burned away our naive focus on model metrics and forced us to start thinking like an engineer of data systems. It was the most expensive and valuable education of our career.

From Projects to Products

Why "Done" is a Four-Letter Word

To survive and thrive in this field, you must make a **critical mindset shift**, and it's the hardest part of the journey for many. You must stop thinking in terms of **projects** and start thinking in terms of **data products**.

- **A Project is a Movie Prop:** It's beautiful, serves a purpose for a scene, and then goes on a shelf. What's the difference? It's everything. A project is like a beautifully crafted movie prop. Think of the hero's sword from a fantasy epic. It's meticulously designed, looks incredible on camera, serves its purpose for a specific scene, and once filming is over, it's put in a display case. It's a static artifact, a testament to a moment in time. A data project is that sword. The output: the analysis, the slide deck, and the pickled model file are "artifacts". It's interesting, it's valuable for a moment, but it's not alive. Its output is a static artifact: a report, a presentation, a model file. It has a defined end.

- **A Data Product is a Battle-Ready Tool:** A data product, on the other hand, is the real, battle-ready tool that the crew uses on set every single day. It's not as glamorous, but it's essential. It must work reliably every time, under changing conditions, and when it breaks, it needs to be fixed immediately because the entire product depends on it. A data product is a living, breathing system. It's a service that other parts of the business depend on, and its value is measured not by how it looks, but by the work it enables. It must work reliably under changing conditions. Its value is measured by ongoing business impact, not a one-time accuracy score.

Let's break down this philosophical divide with the two mindsets.

The Project Mindset (The Waterfall)

The project mindset is the default for most people entering the field, especially from academia. It's linear and finite.

- **The Task:** "Analyze last quarter's sales data to identify drivers of customer churn."
- **The Process:** You receive a static dataset, probably a CSV extract. You perform analysis in a notebook, build an elegant model, and achieve a high accuracy score on the test set.
- **The Output:** A detailed report, a presentation to stakeholders, and perhaps a model object saved to a file, such as the final v3 churn model with new features.pkl.
- **The Outcome:** The project is "done." A collective sigh of relief. The report is insightful, but it's a snapshot of the past. It can't identify a customer who is thinking about leaving *right now*. The insight is static and loses value the moment it's created. The world moves on, but the report doesn't.

The Data Product Mindset (The Loop)

The product mindset is cyclical, operational, and focused on continuous value delivery.

- **The Task:** "Build an automated system to *reduce* customer churn by 5% this year."
- **The Process:** You build a model, sure, but that's just one component. You also build a robust data pipeline that continuously ingests new customer data from multiple sources. You build a system that automatically re-trains and validates the model on a schedule. You wrap the model in a low-latency, scalable API. You add logging, monitoring, and alerting.
- **The Output:** A living, breathing system. A service with an SLA (Service Level Agreement) that other engineering teams can integrate with.
- **The Outcome:** The company's marketing automation platform calls your API daily to get a list of at-risk customers. The platform then automatically triggers a personalized intervention, like an email with a special offer. Success isn't measured by offline accuracy; it's measured by a tangible, observable reduction in the churn rate, "a real business KPI". The system is never "done"; it's continuously monitored, maintained, and improved.

The Project Mindset	The Data Product Mindset
Task: "Analyze last quarter's sales to identify churn drivers."	**Task:** "Build a system to reduce customer churn by 5% this year."
Process: Static CSV → Notebook → Model → Report.	**Process:** Continuous data pipeline → Automated retraining → API → Monitoring.
Output: A presentation and a .pkl file. The project is "done."	**Output:** A live service with an SLA. The system is never "done."
Outcome: Interesting, but static, insight.	**Outcome**: A measurable reduction in churn rate. Continuous value.

Table 1.1. Project Mindset vs. Product Mindset

This isn't just a semantic difference; it's a profound shift in responsibility and organizational politics. A project can often be handled entirely within the data science team. A product, however, requires a cross-functional alliance. You need to negotiate with the data engineering team for pipeline resources. You need to work with the DevOps team to provision infrastructure. You need to align with the software engineering team that will consume your API. You need to convince the product manager that your service deserves a spot on their roadmap. You are no longer just a service provider delivering an artifact; you are a stakeholder, a partner, and an owner. Consider two of the most famous data products in the world:

The Netflix Recommendation Engine

The Netflix recommendation engine is a canonical example of a mature, high-impact data product. It's not a single algorithm but a complex ecosystem of models and infrastructure working together to create a deeply personalized user experience.

The first thing to understand is that Netflix's goal is **not** to predict what star rating you might give a movie. Their primary business metric is **user engagement**, which is a proxy for long-term member retention. The core question the system tries to answer is: "Given the vast library of content, what can they present to a specific user, at this specific moment, that will maximize the chances they find something they love and continue their subscription?"

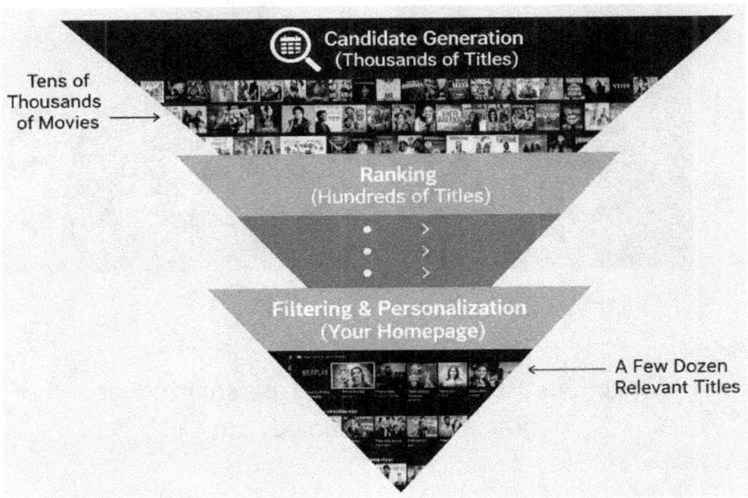

Figure 1.3. The multi-stage funnel of the Netflix recommendation system.

At its core, the recommendation system operates like a sophisticated funnel. It begins with an enormous pool of tens of thousands of potential titles. It progressively narrows them down through multiple intelligent stages until only the most relevant few dozen remain; precisely the ones that matter to you right now.

Stage 1: Candidate Generation (The Long List)

The first stage is deliberately broad. Rather than immediately identifying the absolute best recommendations, its goal is to cast a wide net and surface every plausible candidate that might be of interest. To achieve this, hundreds of different candidate-generation algorithms run in parallel. Some focus on your past viewing or reading history, others on popularity trends, similar users' behavior, content similarity, or even emerging cultural signals. This multi-pronged approach ensures the system generates a large, diverse long list; typically thousands of titles; maximizing recall and minimizing the risk of overlooking hidden gems that a single algorithm might miss.

Figure 1.4. Netflix personalizes artwork to appeal to different user tastes.

By keeping this stage expansive, the system maintains diversity and serendipity while laying a strong foundation for the more precise filtering that follows in subsequent stages.

Each algorithm answers a different kind of question:

- **"Because you watched..." (Collaborative Filtering):** The classic "users who liked Movie A also liked Movie B" logic.
- **Content-Based Filtering:** Finds titles with similar attributes to what you've watched.
- **"Trending Now":** Looks at recent viewing patterns to identify what's currently popular.
- **"Top Picks for You":** A more personalized ranking using your long-term viewing history.
- **"New Releases":** A business-driven model to surface new content.

Stage 2: Ranking (The Short List)

This is where the heavy-duty, personalized machine learning happens. A single, powerful ranking model scores each of the thousands of candidates from Stage 1 for a specific user, predicting the probability that *you* will play a given title. It uses a rich set of features, including your viewing history, the title's metadata, and the current context (like time of day).

Stage 3: Filtering and Personalization (The Final Polish)

The final stage takes the ranked list and applies business rules and additional personalization.

- **Filtering:** It removes titles the user has already seen or content that might be inappropriate for a specific profile.
- **Row and Artwork Personalization:** It decides which rows to show ("Witty Comedies") and even selects the thumbnail artwork for a title that is most likely to appeal to you.

The Tech Stack

Netflix's stack is a mix of open-source technologies and powerful in-house tools, running primarily on AWS.

- **Data Processing: Apache Spark** for massive-scale offline processing and **Apache Flink** for real-time stream processing.
- **Data Storage: Amazon S3** for the data lake and **Cassandra** for key-value storage.

- **Machine Learning: Python** (with **TensorFlow, PyTorch**) for model development, **Java** and **Scala** for high-performance data engineering.
- **Infrastructure and Serving:** A **microservices architecture** using **Docker** containers, served via low-latency APIs on Amazon Web Services (AWS).

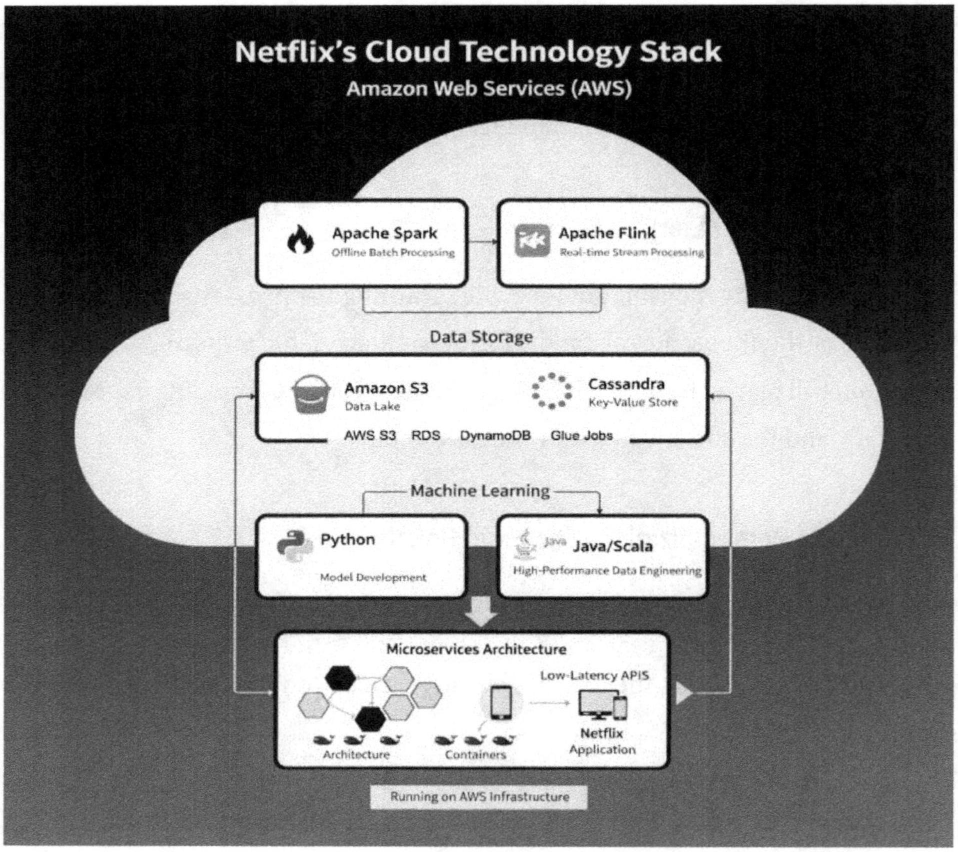

Figure 1.5. Netflix Tech Stack.

Illustrative Code Examples

Example 1: Candidate Generation (SQL)

The query on the next page shows the basic logic for a collaborative filtering candidate generator.

```
— Find other movies watched by users who watched 'The Matrix'
WITH matrix_watchers AS (s
- Step 1: Find all users who watched 'The Matrix'
SELECT user_id FROM viewing_history WHERE title = 'The Matrix'
)
- Step 2: Find all other titles those users watched
SELECT
v.title,
COUNT (DISTINCT v. user_id) AS number_of_watchers
FROM
viewing_history AS v
JOIN
matrix watchers AS m ON v.user_id = m.user_id
WHERE
v.title != 'The Matrix'
GROUP BY
v.title
ORDER BY number_of.
_watchers DESC
LIMIT 100;
```

Listing 1.1: Collaborative filtering candidate generator.

Example 2: Ranking (Python Pseudo-code)

This snippet shows the logic for the ranking stage.

```
import joblib
# In a real system, this model would be loaded from a model registry
# and could be a complex TensorFlow or PyTorch neural network.
ranking_model = joblib.load(' deep_learning_ranker.pkl')
def rank_candidates (user_id, candidate_titles):
"'"Scores a list of candidate titles for a
specific user."""
user_features = get_user_features(user_id) # e.g., viewing history vector
scored_titles = []
for title in candidate_titles:
title_features = get_title_features(title) # e.g., genre vector
feature_vector = combine_features (user_features, title_features)
# Model predicts the probability the user will play this title
play_probability = ranking_model.predict_proba(feature_vector)[0][1]
scored_titles.append((title, play_probability))
# Sort titles by their predicted play probability, highest first
scored_titles.sort (key=lambda x: x[1], reverse=True)
return scored_titles
# --- Example Usage
candidates = ['Inception', 'The Social Network', 'Dune', 'Parasite']
final_ranked_list = rank_candidates (user_id='ankit_anand', candidate_titles=candidates)
print(final_ranked_listl:51)
```

Listing 1.2: Ranking pseudo-code for a recommendation model.

A Bank's Real-Time Fraud Detection System

If the Netflix recommender is a masterclass in driving user engagement, a real-time fraud detection system at a major financial institution is a masterclass in mission-critical, high-stakes decision-making under extreme time constraints. It is a data product where a mistake isn't a bad movie suggestion, but a potentially catastrophic financial loss or a deeply frustrated customer.

The Goal: Speed and Precision Under Pressure

The core business objective is a delicate balancing act. The system must achieve two seemingly contradictory goals simultaneously:

- **Maximize Fraud Detection (High Recall):** It must catch as many fraudulent transactions as possible to minimize financial losses for the bank and its customers.
- **Minimize False Positives (High Precision):** It must avoid declining legitimate transactions. A false positive: declining a customer's valid purchase at a grocery store is a terrible customer experience that can erode trust and lead to churn.

All of this must happen in the blink of an eye. The entire process, from the moment a card is swiped to the decision being sent back to the terminal, must take place in under **100-200 milliseconds.**

The Architecture: A Real-Time Streaming Funnel

Unlike the Netflix system, which has a large offline component, a fraud detection system is overwhelmingly focused on real-time stream processing.

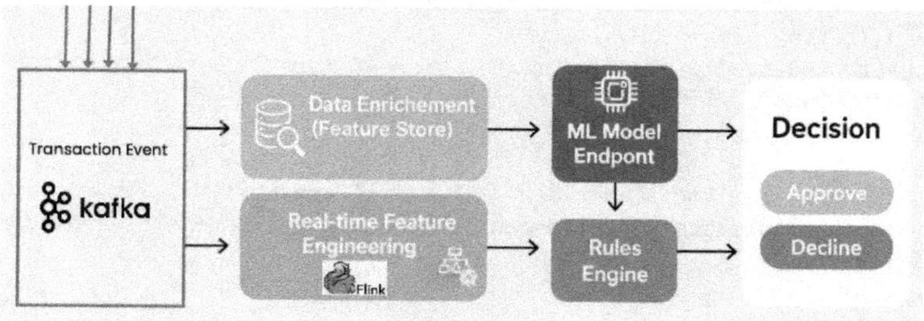

Figure 1.6. The high-level architecture of a real-time fraud detection pipeline.

Stage 1: Event Ingestion and Data Enrichment

The process begins the instant a customer makes a purchase.

- **Event Capture:** The transaction containing data like card number, amount, merchant ID, and location is captured by the bank's core processing system and immediately published to a real-time message broker.

- **Data Enrichment:** The single transaction event is just the tip of the iceberg. To make an intelligent decision, the system must enrich this event with historical context in just a few milliseconds. This involves ultra-fast lookups from a **Feature Store** (often built on an in-memory database like Redis or a low-latency NoSQL store). It fetches pre-calculated features like:

    - The cardholder's average transaction amount.
    - The merchant's typical fraud rate.
    - The last known location of the cardholder.

Stage 2: Real-time Feature Engineering

With the enriched data, the stream processing engine calculates new features on the fly. These are often "velocity checks" that describe behavior over very short time windows.

- How many transactions has this card attempted in the last 10 minutes?
- What is the total dollar amount spent by this user in the last hour?
- Was this card just used in Texas 20 minutes ago, and is now being used in Romania? (An "impossible travel" feature.)

These features are incredibly powerful for detecting common fraud patterns.

Stage 3: Model Inference and Decisioning

The final feature vector, now containing dozens or hundreds of data points, is sent to a low-latency machine learning model endpoint for scoring.

- **Model Scoring:** The ML model (often a highly optimized Gradient Boosting model like LightGBM or a custom neural network) outputs a fraud probability score, from 0 to 1.

- **Rules Engine:** The score is then passed to a business rules engine. This engine provides a final layer of logic and control. For example:

    - IF score > 0.98 THEN auto_decline
    - IF score > 0.80 AND amount > $500 THEN send 2fa push notification
    - IF score < 0.80 THEN auto_approve

This combination of a probabilistic ML model and a deterministic rules engine provides both intelligent prediction and fine-grained business control.

The Tech Stack

The tech stack for these systems is optimized for extreme low latency and high throughput.

- **Event Streaming: Apache Kafka** is the industry standard for the message broker. **Apache Flink** is a top choice for a stream processing engine due to its powerful capabilities for stateful processing and time-window management.

- **Data Storage:** A mix of technologies is used. An in-memory database like **Redis** or **Apache Ignite** for the real-time feature store, and a data lake/warehouse (like Snowflake or a Hadoop- based system) for storing historical data for offline model training.

- **Machine Learning:** While **Python** is used for offline model training and experimentation (using libraries like **XGBoost**, **LightGBM**, and **TensorFlow**), the real-time inference services are often written in high-performance languages like **Java** or **Scala** to minimize latency.

- **Infrastructure:** A **microservices architecture** running on container orchestration platforms like **Kubernetes** or **OpenShift**, often deployed in private or hybrid cloud environments for security and performance reasons.

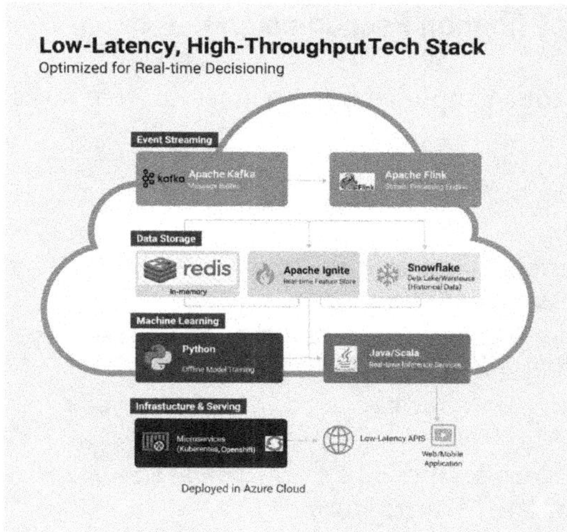

Figure 1.7. High Throughput and Low Latency Architecture's Tech Stack.

Illustrative Code Examples

Example 1: Real-time Feature Engineering (Flink SQL)

This conceptual query demonstrates how you could use Flink SQL to calculate a 10-minute transaction count for each credit card in real time.

```
— This Flink SQL query calculates a real-time feature:
- the number of transactions per card over a 10-minute tumbling window.
SELECT
card_number,
- The windowend time is useful for joining with other features
INTERVAL
TUMBLE_END(transaction_time, INTERVAL '10' MINUTE) as window_end,
COUNT (transaction_id) as transactions_in_last_10_min
FROM
transactions_stream
GROUP BY
- Group by the card number and the time window card_number,
TUMBLE (transaction time, INTERVAL '10' MINUTE):_
```

Listing 1.3: Flink SQL for calculating a 10-minute transaction count in real-time.

Example 2: Inference Service (Python Pseudo-code)

This snippet shows the logic for a simplified inference service that takes a transaction and returns a decision.

```
import redis
# In a real system, these would be connections to live services
fraud_model = load_model ('fraud_model.bin')
feature_store = redis.Redis (host='redis-feature-store.prod', port=6379)
rules_engine = RulesEngine ()
def decide_transaction(transaction: dict) -> dict:
" I"
Scores a transaction for fraud risk in real-time.
card_number = transaction['card_number']
# 1. Enrich data from the real-time feature store
historical_features = feature_store.get(f"card_features:{card_number}")
# 2. Calculate real-time features (in reality, this happens in Flink)
# For this example, we'll just add it to the feature vector.
real_time_features = {'tx_amount': transaction[' amount' ]}
# 3. Combine features and score with the model
feature_vector = {historical_features, real_time_features}
fraud_score = fraud_model.predict_proba(feature_vector) [0][1]
# 4. Apply business rules to the score
decision, reason = rules_engine.apply(fraud_score, transaction)
return {
"transaction_id": transaction['transaction_id'l,
"decision": decision, # e.g., 'APPROVE', 'DECLINE', 'CHALLENGE'
"fraud_score": fraud_score,
"reason": reason
```

Listing 1.4: Pseudo-code for a real-time fraud detection inference service.

The Deployed Data Scientist's Manifesto

Embracing the product mindset requires a new set of guiding principles. This isn't just a checklist; it's a creed that separates a data analyst from a data product owner. Many of you would have learned each of these lessons the hard way.

- **I am an Owner, not just a Builder.** This means when the pager goes off at 2 AM because a data pipeline failed and my model is serving stale predictions, it's my problem. My job doesn't end when the model is trained or the code is committed. I am responsible for its performance, its reliability, and its business impact from conception to retirement. Ownership means caring about uptime, latency, and cost just as much as I care about AUC scores.

- **My Code Lives in Production, Not a Notebook.** I love Jupyter notebooks. They are a phenomenal tool for exploration, visualization, and rapid prototyping. But they are a terrible place for production code to live. The "Black Hole of Jupyter Notebooks" is a real phenomenon in many companies; it's a graveyard of brilliant, one-off analyses that are impossible to reproduce, version, or automate. Production systems demand the discipline of software engineering: version control with Git, code reviews via pull requests, and modular, testable code. We must treat the data science code with the same rigor as any other piece of critical infrastructure.

- **Accuracy is the Start, Not the End.** That 97% accuracy from the churn model story was a siren song, luring us toward the rocks of production failure. A single metric is a dangerously incomplete picture. A successful data product is judged on a balanced scorecard: Does it meet the business objective? (Business Metric). Is it fast enough? (Latency). How much does it cost to run? (Cost). Is it fair and unbiased? (Ethics). Is it reliable? (Uptime). The model must be observable, maintainable, scalable, and secure. Accuracy is just the ticket to the game; it doesn't win it for you.

- **I Build Loops, Not Lines.** A linear process to get data, build a model, and deploy is doomed to fail because it assumes a static world. The world is anything but static. Customer behavior changes, competitors launch new products, and data schemas evolve. My systems must be designed for this reality. I must build continuous loops for feedback, monitoring, and retraining. I assume the world will change and my model will decay; I build the infrastructure to adapt. This is the essence of MLOps.

- **I Speak Business, Not Just Math.** This is the capstone principle that ties everything together. My goal is not to build a complex model; it's to solve a business problem. I must be able to translate the arcane language of p-values, ROC curves, and log-loss into the universal language of business: ROI, operational efficiency, and competitive advantage. My ability to influence decisions is just as important as my ability to build models.

The Data Scientist as a Business Leader

Early in our careers, we made the classic mistake. We walked into a meeting with senior stakeholders from the manufacturing division. We were there to pitch an initiative for improving the vendor master data quality. We were very proud of our work. Our slide deck was a technical masterpiece. We had slides showing data profiles, null value percentages, and the projected increase in data consistency from the proposed deduplication algorithm. We talked about establishing a "golden record" and the beauty of a clean data model. We were met with blank stares and polite nods. Ten minutes in, we could feel the energy draining from the room. They weren't getting it. The Head of Procurement finally cut in, "Son, this is all very interesting, but we have a factory to run. What does any of this have to do with getting parts on time?" He was right. We failed! We were so focused on the technical solution that we forgot to talk about the problem they cared about. We went back to the drawing board. A week later, we were back with a presentation. We were using this simple, powerful framework for every presentation.

The Data Product Leader's Presentation Framework:

- **Slide 1: The Problem.** Quantify the problem in dollars, time, or risk. It had a single, powerful number: the annual cost to the company from shipping delays and incorrect orders caused by having duplicate or incorrect vendor information in the ERP system. It was a seven-figure number. You had their full attention. *Example: "Poor vendor data causes $3 million annually in shipping errors and delays."*

- **Slide 2: The Solution (in plain English).** Describe what you'll build without jargon. You don't mention "deduplication" or "golden records." You said, "We will build a centralized, automated system to ensure that every time they enter a vendor, it's correct and unique.

We project that this will reduce shipping errors by 15% in the first year, saving an estimated $1.2 million.

- **Slide 3: The Impact.** Show the result in business KPIs. The presentation was not just text or numbers, but a visual representation showing the result in business KPIs. *Example: "This will reduce errors by 15%, saving $1.2 million in the first year."*

This framework transforms you from a technical consultant into a strategic partner. The project will be approved on the spot. This teaches a crucial lesson: **the greatest model in the world is useless if you can't get the business to trust, fund, and deploy it**. To do that, you must stop acting like a technical consultant and start acting like a business leader. Instead of starting a conversation with, *"What data do you have?"*, a leader starts with, *"What business decision are you trying to improve?"* or *"What is the most inefficient process on your team?"* This simple rephrasing aligns your work with a tangible goal from day one. When you present your results, frame them with this simple, powerful structure:

- **The Problem You are Solving:** Start with the pain. Quantify it in terms of money, time, or risk.

- **Your Solution (in Plain English):** Describe what you built in terms that a non-technical person can understand. Avoid jargon at all costs.

- **The Impact on the Business:** This is what truly matters. Show the results in the KPIs the business cares about: revenue gained, costs saved, time reduced, or risk mitigated.

The Ethics of Deployment: A Proactive Responsibility

This brings us to the most important mindset shift of all. When your model moves from your laptop to a production server, it ceases to be a mathematical exercise. It becomes an active agent in the world. It makes decisions, and those decisions have consequences. Deploying a model is an act of power, and with that power comes profound responsibility. In the lab, ethics can feel theoretical. In production, they are an imperative.

Algorithmic Bias: The Ghosts in the Data

The most dangerous and pervasive ethical problem is algorithmic bias. This isn't about programmers intentionally writing prejudiced code. It's about models learning from a world that is already full of hidden, systemic biases.

- **Historical Bias:** This is what happened in the famous case of the tech recruiting AI that penalized women's resumes. The model was trained on 10 years of company hiring data, a history in which men were predominantly hired for technical roles. The data was a mirror of a biased past, and the model faithfully learned to replicate it.

- **Selection Bias:** Imagine you build a product recommendation model trained only on data from customers who bought something. The model never learns about users who visited the site, couldn't find what they were looking for, and left. The training data is a biased sample of only the successful outcomes, ignoring the failures.

- **Measurement Bias:** If you train a predictive maintenance model for factory equipment using data from a sensor that is consistently mis-calibrated, the model will learn the sensor's errors as if they were ground truth. The way you measure the world can inject its own bias.

A deployed data scientist must be a proactive auditor. This means rigorously examining data for potential biases *before* training begins, using fairness metrics to test a model's performance across different demographic groups, and implementing de-biasing strategies as part of the production pipeline.

The Framework for Accountability

If your model denies someone a loan, who is responsible? You? The bank? The person who wrote the code? In many legal jurisdictions, "the algorithm did it" is not an acceptable answer. A proactive framework for accountability is non-negotiable.

- **Model Cards:** A crucial practice, pioneered by Google, is the creation of "Model Cards." Think of it as a nutrition label for your model. It's a short, clear document that outlines what the model does, its intended use cases, its performance characteristics (including for different user groups), and crucially, its limitations and ethical considerations. It creates a record of accountability.

- **Human-in-the-Loop (HITL):** For high-stakes decisions, the most responsible architecture is one where the model doesn't make the final call. It acts as a co-pilot, flagging high-risk cases or making recommendations, then sends the case to the expert for review. This isn't a failure of automation; it's a feature of a robust, ethical system.

Transparency and Privacy

In regulated industries like finance and healthcare, a black-box model is a significant liability. If you deny someone credit, regulations like the Equal Credit Opportunity Act (ECOA) in the US require you to provide a reason. This makes transparency and explainability (a topic we will cover in depth in Chapter 7) a legal and business necessity, not just a nice-to-have.

Furthermore, as data scientists, we are stewards of the data we use, much of which is sensitive. Our work in MDM involved handling Personally Identifiable Information (PII) for millions of customers and confidential data for tens of thousands of vendors. Protecting that data is a fundamental responsibility. This means embracing privacy-preserving techniques, robust access controls, and building systems that comply with regulations like GDPR and CCPA from the ground up. We are not just engineers of algorithms; we are architects of the decisions our systems make. This is a profound responsibility. We must embrace it from the very first line of code.

Chapter Summary

This first chapter was about establishing the single most important part of the journey: the mindset. We learned that the skills that make a great analyst are different from those that make a successful deployed data scientist. This is the core philosophy that underpins the rest of the book.

This chapter was the "why." It explained the hard-won lessons that force us to adopt a new, more rigorous discipline for production machine learning.

- **Build Products, Not Projects:** This is the core theme. A "project" ends, and its output is a static artifact. A "product" is a living system that is never truly" done" and must be owned, monitored, and maintained for its entire lifecycle.

- **Real-World Failures are Data Failures:** The "Ghost in the Join" and "Silent Failure" stories taught us that the most catastrophic bugs are often not in the model's algorithm but in the data pipelines that feed it.

- **Speak Business, Not Just Math:** The Deployed Data Scientist's Manifesto reframes the role. We are owners, not just builders. The success is measured by business **ROI**, not just model **accuracy**.

- **MLOps is a Continuous Loop:** We must build systems for continuous feedback, monitoring, and retraining, not a linear path that stops at deployment.

- **Ethics and Responsibility are Production Features:** A deployed model makes real-world decisions.

We are responsible for ensuring our systems are fair, transparent, and auditable from the very first line of code.

CHAPTER 2

Data Strategy: The Lifeblood and Liability of Your Model

In the last chapter, we established a new mindset: a model isn't a project, it's a product. Now, we move from the philosophical to the practical. The first, most critical step in building any successful product is securing your supply chain. In our world, that supply chain is data.

You can have the most sophisticated neural network architecture, the fastest GPUs, and the most elegant CI/CD pipeline in the world, but if the data you feed into it is flawed, your entire system will crumble. It's like putting cheap, dirty fuel into a Formula 1 engine. You won't get high performance; you'll get a catastrophic failure. The "silent failure" with the churn model wasn't a modeling problem; it was a supply chain problem.

This chapter elevates the discussion of data from simple hygiene to a chore you do before the "real work" begins to a strategic imperative. We need to move beyond the common, linear approach of "get data, clean data" and delve into the critical, ongoing process of architecting a robust data ecosystem. Data is not just fuel for your models; it is simultaneously your company's biggest liability and its most valuable asset. How you manage it will define your success or failure as a deployed data scientist.

Beyond the CSV

The Modern Data Ecosystem

In the sheltered world of a Kaggle competition or an academic project, data often arrives as a single, tidy CSV file. It's a clean, static, self-contained snapshot of the world: a perfect specimen for dissection in the lab. Production is never like that. In a real enterprise, data is a sprawling, chaotic, multi-source ecosystem.

Figure 2.1. The evolution of data architecture from warehouses to lakehouse.

A true data professional must be a systems thinker, understanding the purpose, architecture, and strategic trade-offs of components. This isn't just a best practice; it's a matter of survival. Let's walk through the evolution of the core architectural patterns you'll encounter and introduce the key components of the **Modern Data Stack.**

The Data Warehouse: The Organized Library

For decades, the undisputed king of the enterprise data world was the **data warehouse**. Think of it as a meticulously organized central library. It's a repository for structured, historical information, where every piece of data has been cleaned, cataloged, and placed in a specific, predefined location (a schema).

The core principle of the data warehouse is **schema-on-write**. You must define the structure of your data, including the tables, the columns, and the data types, *before* you can write any data into it. The process to get data in is called **ETL (Extract, Transform, Load)**. The "T" (Transform) is the key here. All the messy, complex business logic for cleaning and reshaping the data happens *before* it ever touches the pristine floors of the warehouse. This transformation stage is where classic data warehousing methodologies, such as **Kimball** (building data marts around business processes using dimensional models like the star schema) and **Inmon** (building a highly normalized, centralized enterprise data warehouse), come into play. For analysts, the result is a set of clean, easy-to-query tables, often in a star schema, where a central "fact" table (like sales transactions) is linked to multiple "dimension" tables (like customers, products, and dates).

- **Best For:** BI reporting, historical analysis, and batch-based predictive models where data quality and consistency are paramount.

- **Key Limitation:** The rigidity of schema-on-write makes it slow to adapt to new data sources and unsuitable for unstructured or semi-structured data such as images, logs, or JSON files. The ETL process can be a significant engineering bottleneck.

- **Cloud Platforms:** The major cloud providers offer powerful, managed data warehousing solutions.
    - **Amazon Redshift:** One of the first and most mature cloud data warehouses.
    - **Google BigQuery:** Its serverless architecture and incredible performance on massive SQL queries.
    - **Azure Synapse Analytics:** Microsoft integrates data warehousing with big data analytics.

The Data Lake: The Unfiltered Reservoir

As the "big data" era exploded, the limitations of the data warehouse became glaringly obvious. The volume, velocity, and most importantly, *variety* of data couldn't be forced into the neat rows and columns of a traditional warehouse.

The response was the **data lake**. If the warehouse is an organized library, the data lake is a massive, unfiltered reservoir. The philosophy is completely different: **store everything now, figure out what to do with it later**. You dump data in its raw, native format. The guiding principle is **schema-on-read**. This flips the ETL process into **ELT (Extract, Load, Transform)**.

A crucial technical detail here is the use of analytical file formats. While you can store CSVs in a data lake, for any serious work, you'll use formats like **Apache Parquet** or **Apache ORC**. Unlike row-based CSVs, these are columnar formats. This means that data for each column is stored together, which makes analytical queries that touch only a few columns (like 'SELECT AVG(price) FROM transactions ') exponentially faster, as the query engine doesn't have to read through every other column to find the data it needs. They also offer excellent compression and support schema evolution.

- **Best For:** Exploratory data science, training machine learning models on large and unstructured datasets.
- **Key Limitation:** Without strong governance, a data lake can quickly degenerate into a **data swamp,** a vast, unusable repository of uncatalogued, undocumented, and untrustworthy information.
- **Cloud Platforms:** Data lakes are built on top of cloud object storage.
    - Amazon S3 (Simple Storage Service)
    - Azure Data Lake Storage (ADLS)
    - Google Cloud Storage

Cloud Walkthrough: Snowflake vs. Redshift vs. Big- Query vs. Databricks

Choosing the right data platform is a strategic decision with long-term implications. Here's a practical comparison based on real-world deployments:

Criteria	Snowflake	Amazon Redshift	Google BigQuery	Databricks
Architecture	Multi-cluster, shared data	Massively Parallel Processing (MPP)	Serverless, columnar	Lakehouse platform
Pricing Model	Compute-time Based	Instance-based + storage	Pay-per-query	DBU-based
ML Integration	Snowpark ML	SageMaker integration	Big Query ML	Native ML Run-time
Best For	Enterprise analytics	AWS-centric shops	Ad-hoc analysis	AdvancedML workloads
Performance	Excellent scaling	Good for predictable loads	Instant scaling	Best for complex ML

Table 2.1. Comparison of major cloud data platforms for ML workloads.

The Modern Data Stack: The Best of All Worlds

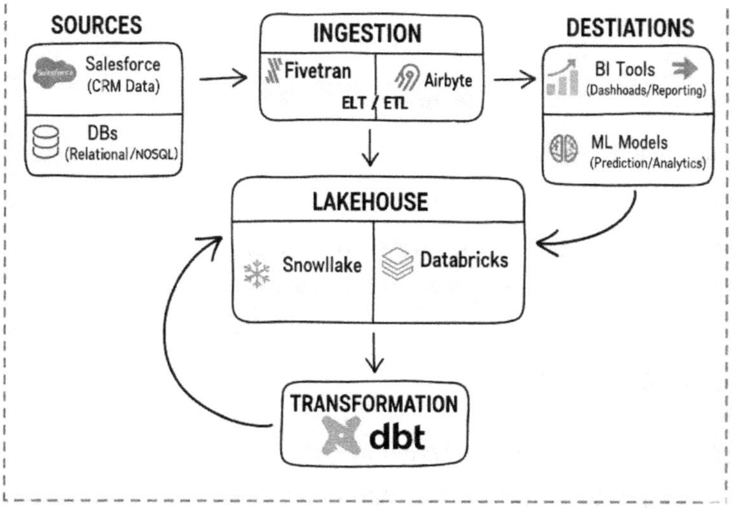

Figure 2.2. Typical Modern Data Stack.

For years, a debate raged: warehouse or lake? Today, that debate is largely over. The industry has converged on a new, best-of-both-worlds architecture commonly called the **Modern Data Stack**. This isn't a single product but a combination of specialized, cloud-native tools that work together. It fully embraces the ELT philosophy. A typical Modern Data Stack has a few key layers:

Ingestion Layer

This layer is all about getting data from your source systems into your data platform with minimal effort.

- **Key Tools**: Tools like **Fivetran** and **Airbyte** have become the standard here. They provide hundreds of pre-built connectors that handle the "E" and "L" (Extract, Load) part of ELT automatically.

Storage and Compute Layer (The Lakehouse)

This is the heart of the modern stack, where the lines between the data lake and data warehouse have blurred into the Lakehouse.

- **Key Tools**: Snowflake and Databricks are the two dominant players. They provide a single platform where you can store massive amounts of raw data and query it with the features of a warehouse. They separate storage from compute, meaning you can scale your processing power up or down independently of how much data you're storing.

The Transformation Layer

This is where the magic happens and represents the biggest shift in modern data strategy. After loading raw data into your Lakehouse, you need to clean, model, and prepare it for analysis.

- **Key Tool: dbt (Data Build Tool)** has completely revolutionized this space. dbt allows anyone comfortable with SQL to perform the "T" (Transform) part of ELT. It brings software engineering best practices like version control, testing, and CI/CD to the world of data modeling. Here is a simple example of what a dbt model looks like. It's just a SQL file.

```
- models/marts/finance/fct_orders.sql
-- This model joins raw order data with raw payment data
- to create a clean, final 'fact' table for analysis.
SELECT
orders.order_id, orders.customer_id, orders.order_date, payments. amount
FROM
{f ref ('stg_orders' ) }} AS orders
LEFT JOIN
{i ref('stg_payments') }} AS payments
ON orders.order_id = payments.payment_order_id
```

Listing 2.1: A dbt model joining orders and payments to create a fact table.

The *{{ ref(...) }}* syntax is dbt's way of managing dependencies between models, automatically creating a reliable data lineage graph.

Field Story: The ETL Rebellion

Once, we were trying to modernize the data infrastructure for one of the e-commerce websites. Their existing system was a classic, four-year-old ETL setup. They had a team of highly specialized ETL developers who used a graphical, drag-and-drop tool. Their process was slow and brittle. If the business analyst wanted a new column added to a report, it would take three weeks. We proposed a move to a modern data stack: **Fivetran** for ingestion, Snowflake as the data platform, and **dbt** for transformations. The idea was met with what we can only describe as a rebellion. The existing BI and ETL teams were deeply skeptical. We decided to prove the concept with a pilot project. Using **Fivetran**, we got the raw Salesforce and Shopify data into **Snowflake** in about an hour. We then worked with a single, frustrated business analyst. Within three days, she had used her SQL skills in dbt to build the exact data model she needed.

The project that would have taken the old team six weeks was done in a fraction of the time, and the business user was now empowered to answer her own questions. The rebellion didn't end overnight, but that small success was the crack in the dam. It demonstrated that the modern approach wasn't about creating chaos; it was about providing governed self-service.

Streaming Architecture: The Central Nervous System

The warehouse, lake, and Lakehouse primarily deal with data at rest. But many of the most valuable data products need to react to events as they happen. This requires a **streaming architecture.** Think of this as a company's central nervous system. It's designed to process a continuous stream of data packets (events) in near real time.

- **Best For:** Real-time fraud detection, live recommendation engines, IoT sensor monitoring.
- **Key Technologies: Apache Kafka** acts as a distributed, persistent log that can ingest millions of events per second.
- **Cloud Platforms:** The major clouds offer managed services like **Amazon Kinesis, Azure Event Hubs**, and **Google Cloud Pub/Sub**.

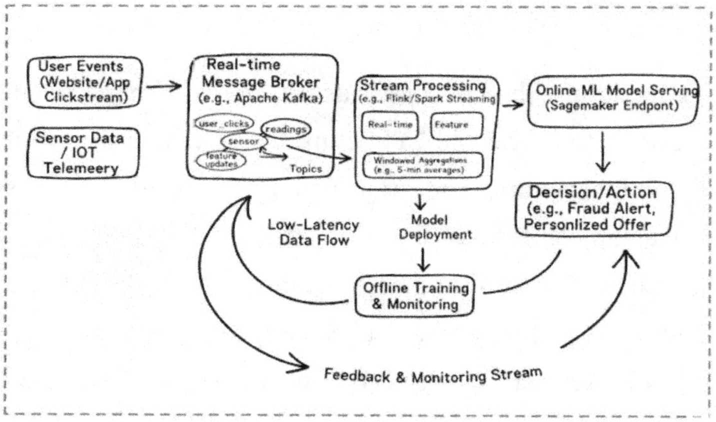

Figure 2.3. Modern Real-Time Streaming ML.

Modern systems increasingly require real-time processing.

Towards Resilient Data Products

In the previous sections, we explored what and *how* of the modern data stack. But the most critical question remains: *why* do so many data initiatives still fail despite having all the right tools? The answer lies not in technology, but in architecture and mindset.

Early in your career, you might be that data engineer working nights and weekends, trapped in dependency chains. The conversation was always the same:

"Is your pipeline running? I can't run mine until yours finishes."
"Why is your SLA my problem? I'm responsible for my pipeline, not yours."

This is the inevitable consequence of **pipeline-first thinking**, where the architect builds their systems around sequential processes rather than business outcomes. They build towers of dependencies where the failure of Pipeline 1 guarantees the failure of Pipelines 2 through N. It's organizational and technical tight coupling masquerading as efficiency.

The fundamental issue isn't that pipelines fail; failure is inevitable in distributed systems. The issue is that they've designed systems that cause failure to cascade. They've built their data infrastructure like dominoes. The root of this problem traces back to a **pre-cloud hangover**. In the data center era, physical hardware was stable, and failures were exceptions. We built systems to handle rare exceptions. But the cloud operates on a completely different principle: **ephemerality**. Virtual machines come and go. The cloud expects things to fail frequently, but in isolated, recoverable ways. When we apply pipeline-first thinking, we're fighting the platform's fundamental nature. We're trying to build rigid, deterministic processes on top of inherently non-deterministic infrastructure. Consider the weather data enrichment example from an e-commerce platform:

```
class DataFirstEnrichmentPipeline:
"""Data-first approach to data enrichment""" def _init__(self):
def
self.data_freshness_threshold = timedelta(hours=1)
enrich_transactions(self, transaction_batch: pd.DataFrame) -> pd.DataFrame:
""Enrich transactions with weather data if available"''
# Check data availability first
latest_weather = self._get_latest_weather_data)
if not self._is_data_fresh(latest_weather):
# Graceful degradation: proceed without enrichment
logging warning( "Weather data stale, proceeding without enrichment")
return transaction_batch
else:
# Data is available, proceed with enrichment
enriched_batch = self._apply_weather_enrichment
transaction_batch, latest_weather
)
return enriched_batch
def
_is_data_fresh(self, weather_data: dict) → bool:
""Check if weather data meets freshness requirements"". if not weather_data or 'timestamp' not in weather_data:
return False
data_timestamp = datetime. fromisoformat(weather_datal' timestamp'])
return (datetime.now() - data timestamp) <= self.data freshness_ threshold_
```

Listing 2.2: Data-first pipeline design with graceful degradation.

The solution is a fundamental mindset shift: from pipeline-first to data-first. Instead of asking ***"Did the previous pipeline succeed?"* We ask, *"Is the data I need available and fresh?"*** This simple shift in approach transforms brittle systems into resilient ones. The enrichment process no longer fails when upstream pipelines fail; it simply waits or degrades gracefully. The system becomes defensive by design. The most powerful implementation of data-first thinking is the strict separation of extraction and transformation. In pipeline-first systems, these are often tightly coupled:

- **Pipeline-First**: Extract → Transform → Load as a single, coupled process.
- **Data-First**: Extract → Load (into raw storage) → Transform (when data is available).

This separation creates natural circuit breakers. Transformation pipelines don't fail because extraction failed; they check whether the required data is available and meets freshness requirements.

This brings us back to data contracts (Section 2.4), but with a new perspective. Data contracts aren't just about quality; they're the foundation of defensive data systems.

```
# Defensive Data Contract Specification
contract_id: 'urn: ecommerce:weather_data:v2' defensive_requirements:
freshness:
max_age_minutes: 60
sla: "99.5%"
"99.5%" # Fresh data available 99.5% of the time
availability:
expected_downtime_minutes_per_week: 30
grace_period_minutes: 120
# How long to wait before alerting
# Defensive consumption patterns
consumption_guidelines:
- "Check data freshness before processing"
- "Proceed with graceful degradation when stale"
- "Never fail catastrophically due to missing upstream data"_
```

Listing 2.3: Data contract with freshness and availability guarantees.

Let us look at how we applied these principles to the seasonal recommendation engine from Section 2.3. Our initial pipeline-first design looked like this:

```
# Pipeline-First Approach (Problematic)
def run_daily_recommendations():
user_behavior = extract_user_behavior ()# Step 1_
product_catalog = extract_product_catalog()#Step 2
inventory_data = extract_inventory ()# Step 3
# All three must succeed or entire pipeline fails
features = build_features(user_behavior, product_catalog, inventory_data)
recommendations = generate_recommendations (features)
load_recommendations (recommendations)
```

Listing 2.4: Initial brittle pipeline design.

When any of the three extraction steps failed, the entire recommendation process failed. We were constantly firefighting. We redesigned it with data-first principles:

```
class ResilientRecommendationSystem:
"''"Data-first recommendation system with graceful degradation"""
def refresh_recommendations (self):
   "'"Refresh recommendations using available data"'"
   # Check what data is actually available
   available_data = self._check_data_availability()
   # Build features with whatever data we have
   features = self._build_features_with_available_data(available_data)
   # Generate recommendations based on available features
   recommendations = self._generate_recommendations (features)
   # Log what we're missing for operational awareness
   if not available_datal 'inventory']:
      logging. info( "Generating recommendations without inventory data")
      self._publish_recommendations(recommendations)
def _check_data_availability(self) - dict:
   "'"Check availability and freshness of all data sources""'"
   return {
      'user_behavior': self._get_fresh_user_behavior(),
      'product_catalog': self._get_fresh_product_catalog(),
      'inventory': self._get_fresh_inventory_data()
   }
```

Listing 2.5: Resilient data-first recommendation system.

The result was transformative. The recommendation system became resilient to failures of individual components. If inventory data were stale, they'd generate recommendations based solely on user behavior and product data. The system continued providing value even when parts of it were temporarily impaired.

The Organizational Impact

This technical shift enables a cultural one. When you stop thinking in terms of pipelines and start thinking in terms of data products:

- **Teams become autonomous:** They depend on data contracts, not pipeline schedules.
- **Failure becomes localized:** Issues don't cascade across team boundaries.
- **Innovation accelerates:** Teams can experiment without fear of breaking dependent systems.

Your architecture reflects your organization. Pipeline-first thinking creates siloed teams and brittle systems. Data-first thinking creates collaborative teams and resilient systems. In the next section, we'll explore how to build the cultural foundation that makes this technical approach sustainable. Because the most elegant data architecture will fail without the right human systems to support it.

The Philosophy of Model Decay: Why All Models Are Born to Fail

Understanding the data ecosystem is the first step. The next is to internalize a sobering truth: in a dynamic world, **all models are born to fail**. A model trained on data from one point in time is a snapshot of a world that no longer exists. Its performance will inevitably degrade as the underlying data and its relationships change. This phenomenon, known as **model drift**, is the single greatest threat to a deployed model's long-term success. I like to think of a model as a map. A map is a perfect representation of the world on the day it was printed. But over time, new roads are built, and cities change. The map hasn't become "wrong"; it has become "outdated." The same is true for your model. The code doesn't change, but the world it operates in does. There are three primary forms of this decay:

Data Drift: When the World Changes Around Your Model

This occurs when the statistical properties of your input data change over time. The fundamental relationship between your features and the target variable remains the same, but the incoming data *looks* different.

Example: A credit scoring model is trained on a dataset of loan applicants primarily from California. The company then expands to serve customers in rural Mississippi, where the cost of living and average incomes are much lower. When the model sees an applicant with a $50,000 income, it flags them as high-risk, even though that income might be very stable in their local context. The model's logic isn't broken, but the distribution of the input data has drifted. Data drift occurs when the statistical properties of input data change over time. Your model was trained on one distribution, but now it's seeing another.

```
import numpy as np
from scipy import stats
from scipy.spatial.distance import jensenshannon
import pandas as pd
class DataDriftDetector:
    """Monitor and detect data drift in production"""
    def __init__(self, reference_data: pd.DataFrame):
        self.reference_data = reference_data
        self.drift_threshold = 0.1  # JS divergence threshold
    def detect_drift(self, current_data: pd.DataFrame) -> dict:
        """Detect drift between reference and current data"""
        drift_report = {}
        for column in self.reference_data.columns:
            if self.reference_data[column].dtype in ['float64', 'int64']:
                # For numerical columns, use KS test
                stat, p_value = stats.ks_2samp(
                    self.reference_data[column].dropna(),
                    current_data[column].dropna()
                )
                drift_report[column] = {
                    'test': 'ks_test',
                    'statistic': stat,
                    'p_value': p_value,
                    'drift_detected': p_value < 0.05
                }
            else:
                # For categorical, use JS divergence
                ref_counts = self.reference_data[column].value_counts(normalize=True)
                curr_counts = current_data[column].value_counts(normalize=True)
            # Align distributions
            all_categories = set(ref_counts.index) | set(curr_counts.index)
            ref_dist = np.array([ref_counts.get(cat, 0) for cat in all_categories])
            curr_dist = np.array([curr_counts.get(cat, 0) for cat in all_categories])
            js_distance = jensenshannon(ref_dist, curr_dist)
            drift_report[column] = {
                'test': 'js_divergence',
                'distance': js_distance,
                'drift_detected': js_distance > self.drift_threshold
                }
        return drift_report
```

Listing 2.6: Detecting data drift with statistical tests.

Concept Drift

This is a much more serious problem. It means the very relationship between your input features and the target variable has changed. The model's fundamental assumptions about the world are no longer valid. **Example**: An e-commerce model learns that the more time a user spends on a product page, the more likely they are to buy. Then, a new privacy law is enacted, and the company must now display a prominent cookie consent banner. Many users now spend the first 10 seconds of their visit looking for the "reject all" button. The relationship between "time spent on page" and "likelihood to buy" has now fundamentally changed. The old model's core assumption is now broken.

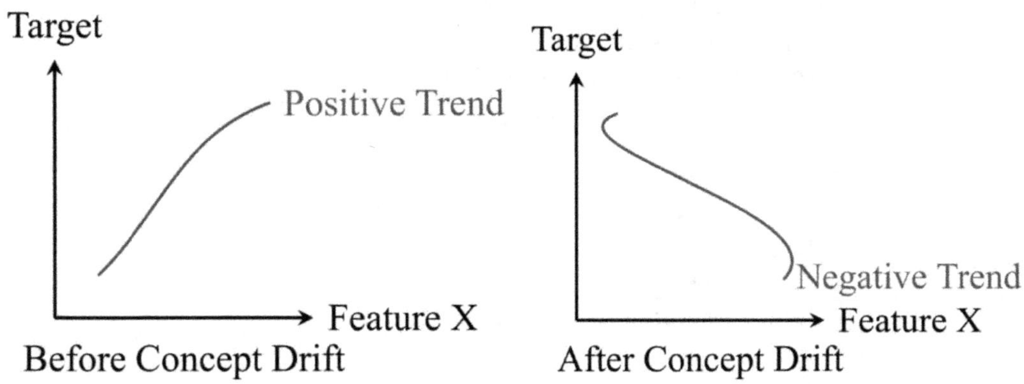

Figure 2.4. Concept drift is shown with trend lines.

Prediction Drift (Operational Drift)

This is a drift in the model's output distribution. It's often a symptom of one of the two drifts above. **Example**: A sentiment analysis model for social media posts normally predicts a 60% positive, 30% neutral, and 10% negative split. Suddenly, your monitoring shows the output has shifted to 80% negative. The model itself isn't necessarily broken, but this is a massive signal that something in the world has changed (e.g., a product recall or a PR crisis). It's the canary in the coal mine. We will dive much deeper into detecting and mitigating drift in Chapter 6, but you must adopt the mindset that your models are temporary now.

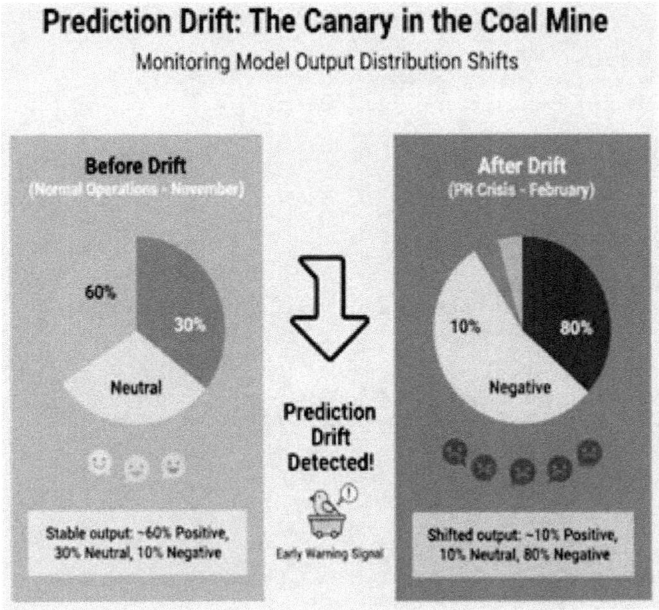

Figure 2.5. Prediction Drift in Coal Mine.

Python Code: Simulating Prediction Drift

The code on the following page simulates a scenario where a sentiment analysis model's output distribution shifts significantly, a phenomenon known as prediction drift. It then uses a Chi-Square statistical test to detect this change.

Field Story: When Seasons Change

A lead data architect at a manufacturing company helped build a sophisticated recommendation engine that analyzed customer browsing behavior using Mastered Customer Data from EBX, along with their purchase history and product attributes, in the analytical system. After months of development, they launched with great fanfare.

```
import numpy as np
import pandas as pd
from scipy.stats import chisquare
# – 1. Simulate Baseline Predictions (Normal Operations) --
# For a sentiment model: 60% Positive, 30% Neutral, 10% Negative
n_samples = 1000
np.random.seed(42)
baseline_preds = np.random.choice(
    ['Positive', 'Neutral', 'Negative'],
    size=n_samples,
    p=[0.60, 0.30, 0.10]
)
# Calculate observed frequencies for baseline
baseline_counts = pd.Series(baseline_preds).value_counts(normalize=True).sort_index()
print("--- Baseline Prediction Distribution –")
print(baseline_counts)
print("-" * 40)
# – 2. Simulate Drifted Predictions (e.g., during a PR crisis) -
# Suddenly, the output shifts to 10% Positive, 10% Neutral, 80% Negative
drifted_preds = np.random.choice(
    ['Positive', 'Neutral', 'Negative'],
    size=n_samples,
    p=[0.10, 0.10, 0.80]
)
# Calculate observed frequencies for drifted data
drifted_counts = pd.Series(drifted_preds).value_counts(normalize=True).sort_index()
print("-- Drifted Prediction Distribution (Post-Crisis) —")
print(drifted_counts)
print("-" * 40)
# – 3. Detect Drift using Chi-Square Test -
# We want to see if the drifted distribution is significantly different from the baseline.
# For chisquare, we need observed and expected *counts*, not percentages.
# Get counts, ensuring consistent order of categories
categories = ['Negative', 'Neutral', 'Positive'] # Ensure consistent order
baseline_actual_counts = pd.Series(baseline_preds).value_counts().reindex(categories, fill_value=0)
drifted_actual_counts = pd.Series(drifted_preds).value_counts().reindex(categories, fill_value=0)
print(f"Baseline Counts: {baseline_actual_counts.tolist()}")
print(f"Drifted Counts: {drifted_actual_counts.tolist()}")
# Perform Chi-Square Test
# Null Hypothesis (HØ): The observed distribution (drifted) is the same as the expected (baseline).
# Alternative Hypothesis (H1): The observed distribution is different.
chi2_stat, p_value = chisquare(f_obs=drifted_actual_counts, f_exp=baseline_actual_counts)
print(f"\n--- Chi-Square Test for Prediction Drift —")
print(f"Chi-square Statistic: {chi2_stat:.2f}")
print(f"P-value: {p_value:.3f}")
# Interpret the p-value
alpha = 0.05
if p_value < alpha:
    print(f"Conclusion: Since p-value ({p_value:.3f}) < alpha ({alpha}), we reject the null hypothesis.")
    print("There is a statistically significant prediction drift.")
else:
    print(f"Conclusion: Since p-value ({p_value:.3f}) >= alpha ({alpha}), we fail to reject the null hypothesis.")
    print("No significant prediction drift detected.")
```

Listing 2.7: Simulating and detecting prediction drift using a Chi-Square test.

The Perfect Storm

The model performed beautifully through the holiday season. Their precision@10 metric hovered around 85%, and business stakeholders were thrilled. But as winter turned to spring, something strange happened. Their performance metrics began a slow, steady decline. By mid-April, precision had dropped to 62%. Customer complaints about irrelevant recommendations poured in. The business team was confused; had they broken something in a recent deployment?

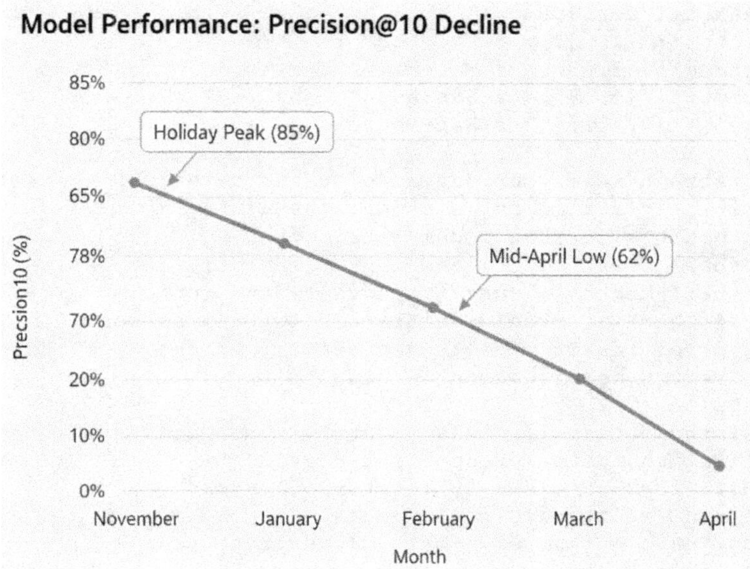

Figure 2.6. Decline in Sales.

They spent days reviewing their code, infrastructure, and data pipelines. Everything was working perfectly. Then, looking at the feature distributions, he noticed: the model was still recommending winter coats and heavy sweaters to customers who were clearly shopping for spring attire.

The problem wasn't in their code; it was in their training data. They had trained the model exclusively on data from October through January, the winter shopping season. The model had never seen spring shopping patterns.

The Solution: Seasonal Model Retraining

They implemented a seasonal retraining strategy:

```
import pandas as pd
from datetime import datetime, timedelta
from models.recommendation import RecommendationModel
class SeasonalRetrainingPipeline:
    """Automated retraining based on seasonal patterns"""
    def __init__(self):
        self.seasonal_periods = {
            'winter': (12, 2), # Dec-Feb
            'spring': (3, 5),  # Mar-May
            'summer': (6, 8),  # Jun-Aug
            'fall': (9, 11)    # Sep-Nov
        }
    def should_retrain(self, current_model_date: datetime) -> bool:
        """Check if it's time for seasonal retraining"""
        current_month = current_model_date.month
        for season, (start_month, end_month) in self.seasonal_periods.items():
            if start_month <= current_month <= end_month:
                # Check if model was trained in this season
                model_season = self._get_season(current_model_date)
                return model_season != season
        return False
    def get_training_data(self, season: str) -> pd.DataFrame:
        """Get training data for specific season"""
        # Use data from same season in previous years
        current_year = datetime.now().year
        training_years = [current_year - 1, current_year - 2]
        seasonal_data = []
        for year in training_years:
            data = self._load_seasonal_data(year, season)
            seasonal_data.append(data)
        return pd.concat(seasonal_data)
    def retrain_model(self, model, new_season: str):
        """Retrain model with seasonal data"""
        training_data = self.get_training_data(new_season)
        retrained_model = model.retrain(training_data)
        return retrained_model
```

Listing 2.8: Seasonal model retraining pipeline.

The Outcome

They implemented automatic seasonal retraining and performance monitoring. The system now detects when they're entering a new shopping season and automatically re-trains the model with appropriate historical data. Their precision metrics stabilized, and they never again faced seasonal performance degradation.

The Necessary Guardrails

If data strategy is about building a robust supply chain, then data governance is about ensuring the supply chain is safe, secure, and trustworthy. Good governance isn't about slowing things down; it's about enabling speed and innovation *safely*. I learned this lesson in the most visceral way possible during my time architecting a multi-tenant MDM solution on AWS. A junior developer, working late one night, changed an access policy on a non-production S3 bucket to make a file publicly readable to test a connection. He forgot to change it back. An automated AWS Config rule detected the change within minutes, triggered a Lambda function to revert the policy, and sent a high-priority alert. What could have been a disaster was caught and remediated instantly. Let's break down the core pillars of practical, modern data governance.

Pillar 1: Data Contracts

The silent failures we discussed in Chapter 1 were, at their core, a result of broken or non-existent agreements between data producers and data consumers. The modern solution to this is the **Data Contract**: a formal, machine-readable agreement that defines the schema, semantics, and service-level agreements (SLAs) for a dataset. A data contract, often defined in a YAML file and checked into Git, would include:

- Schema definition (e.g., 'customer ID' is a non-null integer).
- Data quality checks (e.g., 'customer ID' must exist in the master customer table).
- Service levels (e.g., this data will be updated daily by 8 AM).

If the producing system attempts to make a change that violates the contract (e.g., renaming 'customer ID' to 'clv'), the change is automatically blocked in the CI/CD pipeline, preventing a downstream failure before it ever occurs. This is a profound shift from reactive data quality to proactive, producer- driven guarantees.

YAML Data Contract Example (with Specific Constraints)

This document provides a YAML data contract example that incorporates three specific constraints: a schema definition, a data quality check for referential integrity, and a service level agreement for data freshness.

Data Contract: analytics. derived.customer activity_

```
# Data Contract Specification v1.0
contract_id: 'urn:ecommerce-corp:customer_activity:v1'
status: active
owner: 'analytics-eng@ecommerce-corp.com'
dataset:
  name: "analytics.derived.customer_activity"
  description: "A daily summary of customer activities."
# 1. Schema Definition Constraint
schema:
  - name: activity_id
    type: string
    constraints:
      - notnull
      - unique
  - name: customer_id
    type: integer
    description: "Identifier for the customer."
    constraints:
      - not_null
  - name: activity_date
    type: date
    constraints:
      - not_null
  - name: total_sessions
    type: integer
# 2. Data Quality Checks Constraint
quality_checks:
  - type: referential_integrity
    description: "Ensures customer_id exists in the master customer table."
    column: customer_id
    references_table: "prod.main.customers"
    references_column: "id"
# 3. Service Levels Constraint
sla:
  update_schedule: "daily"
  update_deadline: "08:00 UTC"
  description: "This data will be refreshed and available every day by 8 AM UTC."
  availability: "99.5%"
```

Listing 2.9: YAML data contract with schema, quality, and SLA constraints.

How the Constraints Are Met

- **Schema Definition:** The schema section explicitly defines the customer ID data type as an integer and includes NOT NULL as a constraint.
- **Data Quality Checks:** The quality checks section implements the referential integrity rule. It specifies that the customer ID column in this dataset must reference a valid entry in the ID column of the prod. main.customer's table.
- **Service Levels:** The SLA (Service Level Agreement) section defines the data delivery promise. The update deadline is set to "08:00 UTC" under a daily schedule, formally documenting that the data will be updated by 8 AM every day.

Pillar 2: Access Control

This is the foundational principle of all security: people and systems should have access only to the data and resources they absolutely need to do their jobs, and nothing more. Here is an example of a well-scoped AWS IAM policy for an application that only needs to read from a specific S3 bucket:

```
{
    "Version": "2012-10-17",
    "Statement": [
        {
            "Effect": "Allow",
            "Action": "s3:GetObject",
            "Resource": "arn:aws:s3:::my-production-data-bucket/*"
        }
    ]
}
```

Listing 2.10: AWS IAM policy demonstrating the Principle of Least Privilege.

Pillar 3: Data Security and Secrets Management

Protecting your data involves two states of being:

1. **Encryption at Rest:** Your data inside the vault.
2. **Encryption in Transit:** Your armored car.

The cloud providers have made this so easy that there is simply no excuse not to use it. A critical, related practice is secrets management. Your code needs secrets: database passwords, API keys, etc., to function. Never, ever, hardcode these. Use a dedicated service like AWS Secrets Manager, Azure Key Vault, or HashiCorp Vault.

Practical PII Anonymization

```
import hashlib
import re
from faker import Faker
import pandas as pd
class PIIAnonymizer:
    """Anonymize PII in datasets while preserving utility for ML"""
    def __init__(self, salt='company-specific-salt'):
        self.salt = salt
        self.faker = Faker()
    def hash_identifier(self, value: str) -> str:
        """Hash identifiers consistently for linkage"""
        if not value:
            return ""
        return hashlib.sha256(f"{value}{self.salt}".encode()).hexdigest()[:16]
    def anonymize_email(self, email: str) -> str:
        """Replace email with consistent fake email"""
        if not email or '@' not in email:
            return ""
        username, domain = email.split('@')
        hashed_username = self.hash_identifier(username)
        return f"{hashed_username}@example.com"
    def generalize_age(self, age: int) -> str:
        """Generalize age into buckets"""
        if age < 18:
            return "under_18"
        elif age < 26:
            return "18-25"
        elif age < 36:
            return "26-35"
        elif age < 46:
            return "36-45"
        else:
            return "over_45"
    def anonymize_dataset(self, df: pd.DataFrame) -> pd.DataFrame:
        """Apply anonymization to entire dataset"""
        anonymized_df = df.copy()
        if 'email' in df.columns:
            anonymized_df['email'] = df['email'].apply(self.anonymize_email)
        if 'age' in df.columns:
            anonymized_df['age_group'] = df['age'].apply(self.generalize_age)
            anonymized_df = anonymized_df.drop('age', axis=1)
        return anonymized_df
```

Listing 2.11: PII anonymization for ML datasets.

GDPR/CCPA Compliance Framework

```
from datetime import datetime, timedelta
import logging
class DataComplianceManager:
    """Manage GDPR/CCPA compliance for ML systems"""
    def __init__(self, retention_days=730):  # 2 years default
        self.retention_days = retention_days
    def process_deletion_request(self, user_id: str):
        """Process user data deletion request (Right to be Forgotten)"""
        # Delete from databases
        self._delete_user_data('main_database', user_id)
        self._delete_user_data('analytics_database', user_id)
        # Delete from data lakes
        self._delete_from_data_lake(user_id)
        # Update model training to exclude user
        self._retrain_models_without_user(user_id)
        logging.info(f"Completed deletion request for user {user_id}")
    def export_user_data(self, user_id: str) -> dict:
        """Export all data for a user (Data Portability Right)"""
        user_data = {
            'profile': self._get_user_profile(user_id),
            'interactions': self._get_user_interactions(user_id),
            'predictions': self._get_user_predictions(user_id),
            'model_usage': self._get_model_usage(user_id)
        }
        return user_data
    def enforce_data_retention(self):
        """Automatically delete data past retention period"""
        cutoff_date = datetime.now() - timedelta(days=self.retention_days)
        self._delete_old_data(cutoff_date)
```

Listing 2.12: Data compliance framework for GDPR/CCPA.

Building a Data-First Culture

This brings us to the final, and most challenging, part of data strategy. You can have the most elegant Lakehouse architecture and the most secure governance framework in the world. Still, if your organization's culture doesn't support a data-driven mindset, your efforts will ultimately fail.

Pillar 1: Data Literacy and Overcoming Silos

In almost every company you will or have worked with, it's the same pattern. Marketing has its customer data, Sales has theirs, and Finance has theirs. The first step is often just getting people to agree on a common definition for "customer." This requires executive sponsorship and a commitment to treating data as a shared, enterprise-wide asset.

Pillar 2: Clear Ownership and the Data Catalog

A data-first culture establishes clear **data ownership**. This means for every critical data domain, there is a team formally accountable for its quality and maintenance.

- **Data Product Owners**: Each dataset has a designated owner responsible for quality and availability.
- **Service Level Objectives (SLOs)**: Clear metrics for data freshness, completeness, and accuracy.
- **Data Quality Dashboards**: Real-time monitoring of key data quality metrics.
- **Cross-Functional Data Councils**: Regular meetings between business and technical stakeholders.

This is where a Data Catalog becomes essential. Tools like Alation act like a Google for your company's data. They ingest metadata from all your data sources and provide a single place to discover datasets, see who owns them, understand their lineage, and see how they are used. A good data catalog is the technology that underpins a culture of data ownership and trust.

Pillar 3: The Proactive Feedback Loop

Your deployed models are not just consumers of data; they are incredibly powerful producers of feedback about the health of your company's data pipelines. Let's use a concrete example from our time working with an HVAC company. They had a logistics model designed to predict shipment delivery times. Their monitoring system consistently flagged late deliveries due to incorrect zip codes entered into the order entry system.

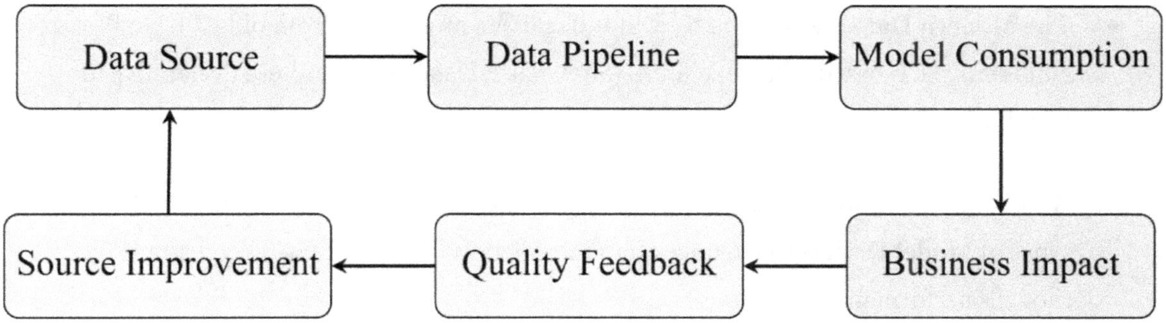

Figure 2.7. The data quality feedback loop: Continuous improvement from consumption back to source.

- **The Old Way (Siloed Culture):** The data science team would have been tasked with building a complex cleaning script.
- **The New Way (Data-First Culture):** We treated this insight as a high-value feedback signal. We took the report to the team that owned the order entry application. We showed them the direct financial impact. Within a week, we implemented real-time zip code validation in the user interface. The bad data stopped flowing at the source.

By building these proactive feedback loops, you transform your models from passive analytical tools into active agents of operational improvement. You're not just analyzing the business; you're helping to fix it. This completes the journey through data strategy. It's a socio-technical discipline. It requires robust architecture and secure governance, but most importantly, a culture of shared ownership and collaboration. With this foundation in place, we are finally ready to do what most people think of as the core of data science: building the model itself.

Chapter Summary

This chapter established the most critical part of the entire MLOps system: the data strategy. We learned that a model is only as good as the data it's fed, and that most production failures are, in fact, data failures. This is "Step Zero" of the MLOps lifecycle.

We moved from thinking of data as a simple CSV to seeing it as a complex, living supply chain. Our goal is to build a resilient data ecosystem, not just brittle pipelines.

- **The Modern Data Stack is the New Standard:** We must move from old ETL paradigms to a modern, ELT-based data Lakehouse (Snowflake, Databricks) and use declarative tools like dbt to manage transformations.
- **All Models Are Born to Fail:** We must build for decay. We learned to identify the three types of **Model Drift** (Data, Concept, and Prediction) that will inevitably degrade our model's performance over time.
- **Data Contracts are Your Best Defense:** To prevent pipeline failures, we must implement **Data Contracts;** an explicit, machine-readable agreement between data producers and consumers that enforces schema and data quality.
- **Data Governance is a Socio-Technical Problem:** A data-first culture is built on the pillars of governance. Tools like **Data Catalogs** (e.g., Alation) and clear **Data Ownership** are essential for breaking down data silos and building trust.

CHAPTER 3

Forging Production-Ready Models

The traditional CRISP-DM framework served us well for analytical projects, but the production machine learning demands a more dynamic, iterative approach. The modern model development lifecycle is a continuous cycle of improvement, validation, and deployment. CRISP-ML(Q) extends CRISP-DM with crucial production considerations:

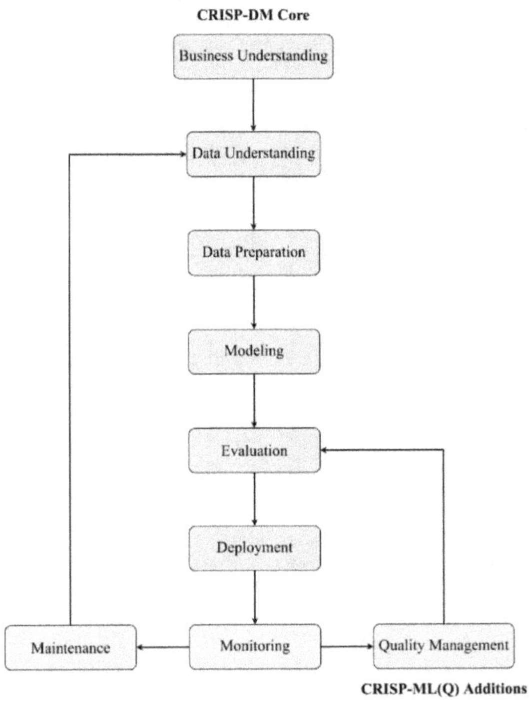

Figure 3.1. CRISP-ML(Q) implementation framework with quality gates.

Professional model development requires systematic experiment tracking:

```
class CRISPDMProject:
    """Example implementation of CRISP-DM phases for retail analytics"""
    def business_understanding(self):
        """Phase 1: Business Understanding"""
        return {
            'business_objectives': [
                "Increase customer retention by 15%",
                "Reduce marketing costs by targeting high-value customers"
            ],
            'success_criteria': [
                "Churn rate reduction from 10% to 8.5%",
                "ROI on marketing campaigns > 300%"
            ],
            'project_constraints': [
                "Budget: $50,000",
                "Timeline: 3 months",
                "Data availability: Customer transaction history"
            ]
        }
    def data_understanding(self, raw_data):
        """Phase 2: Data Understanding"""
        analysis = {
            'data_sources': 'raw_data',
            'data_quality_report': 'generated from data',
            'initial_insights': self._exploratory_analysis(raw_data)
        }
        return analysis
    def data_preparation(self, raw_data):
        """Phase 3: Data Preparation"""
        prepared_data = {
            'cleaned_data': self._handle_missing_values(raw_data),
            'feature_engineered': self._create_features(raw_data),
            'train_test_split': self._split_data(raw_data)
        }
        return prepared_data
    def modeling(self, prepared_data):
        """Phase 4: Modeling"""
        models = {
            'candidate_models': self._train_multiple_models(prepared_data),
            'hyperparameter_tuning': self._optimize_parameters(),
            'model_evaluation': self._evaluate_models()
        }
        return models
    def evaluation(self, models, business_criteria):
        """Phase 5: Evaluation"""
        evaluation_report = {
            'technical_performance': self._assess_model_performance(models),
            'business_alignment': self._check_business_alignment(models, business_criteria),
            'deployment_recommendation': self._make_deployment_decision()
        }
        return evaluation_report
    def deployment(self, selected_model):
        """Phase 6: Deployment"""
        deployment_plan = {
            'integration_approach': "API-based real-time scoring",
            'monitoring_framework': self._create_monitoring_plan(),
            'maintenance_schedule': "Monthly retraining",
            'documentation': self._generate_documentation(selected_model)
        }
        return deployment_plan
```

Listing 3.1: Comprehensive experiment tracking with MLflow for full reproducibility.

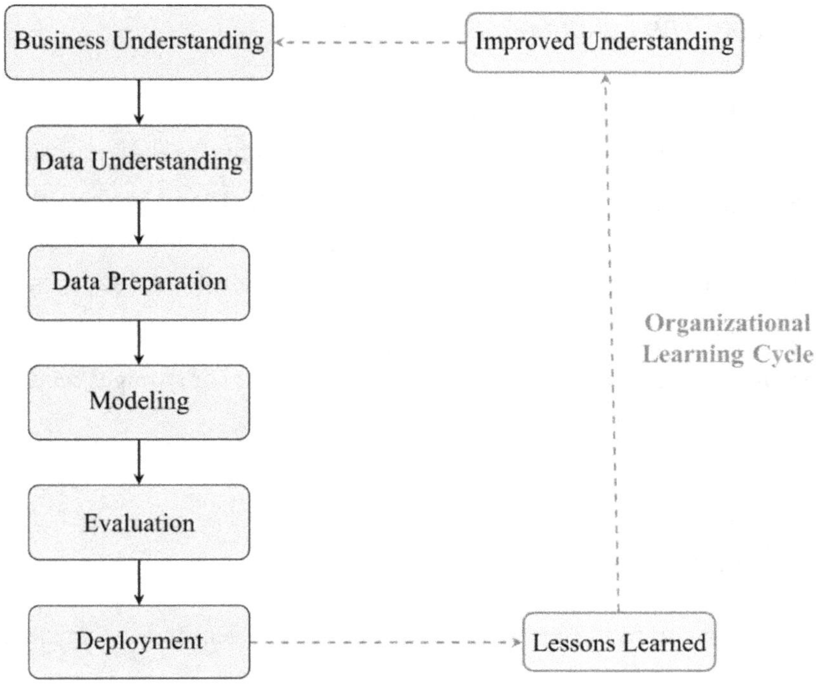

Figure 3.2. The Critical Feedback Loop: Lessons Learned in CRISP-DM.

Strategic Model Selection

Model selection is a multi-dimensional optimization problem balancing technical requirements, business constraints, and operational realities.

Computational Complexity Analysis

Computational complexity analysis measures how much time and memory an algorithm requires to solve a problem as the size of the input grows. It's not about calculating the exact runtime in seconds but rather understanding how an algorithm's performance *scales*. Think of it like searching for a name in a phone book. If you must flip through every single page one by one, your search time grows directly with the number of pages. If you can use the alphabetical order to jump to the right section (like a binary search), your search time grows much more slowly, even if the phone book gets twice as thick. Complexity analysis is the formal way of describing these different growth rates.

Big O Notation: The Language of Complexity

The most common tool for this analysis is **Big O notation**. It describes the *worst-case scenario* for an algorithm's performance, focusing on the most dominant factor, as the input size (represented by n) becomes very large. It simplifies analysis by ignoring constants and less significant terms.

- **Time Complexity**: Measures how the number of operations (and thus, the runtime) scales with the input size n.
- **Space Complexity**: Measures how the amount of memory (or storage) required scales with the input size n.

Common Complexity Classes

Here are some of the most common Big O classes, from most efficient to least efficient.

Model Type	Training Complexity	Inference Complex	Memory	Parallelization
Linear Models	$O(n*d)$	$O(d)$	Low	Excellent
Random Forest	$O(n*d*\log(n)*t)$	$O(d*t)$	Medium	Excellent
Gradient Boosting	$O(n*d*t)$	$O(d*t)$	Medium	Good
Neural Networks	$O(n*d*l*e)$	$O(d*l)$	High	Excellent
Support Vector Machines	$O(n^2*d)$ to $O(n^3*d)$	$O(s*d)$	High	Poor

Note: n=samples, d=features, t=trees, l=layers, e=epochs, s=support vectors.

Table 3.1. Computational complexity of common model types.

- O(1) **Constant Time:** The algorithm takes the same amount of time regardless of the input size. *Example*: Accessing an element in an array by its index (e.g., my array[5]).

- O(log n) **Logarithmic Time:** The time it takes increases very slowly as the input size grows. Doubling the input size doesn't double the work. *Example*: A binary search in a sorted array.

- $O(n)$ **Linear Time:** The runtime grows in direct proportion to the input size. *Example*: Finding an item in an unsorted list by checking each element one by one.

- $O(n \log n)$ **Log-Linear Time:** A very common and efficient complexity for sorting algorithms that scales well. *Example*: Efficient sorting algorithms like Merge Sort or Quicksort.

- $O(n^2)$ **Quadratic Time:** The runtime grows by the square of the input size, often seen with nested loops. Performance degrades quickly. *Example*: Comparing every element in a list to every other element.

- $O(2^n)$ **Exponential Time:** The runtime doubles with each addition to the input size. These algorithms become unusable for even moderately sized inputs; for *example*, brute-force solutions to complex problems like the Traveling Salesperson Problem.

Why Does It Matter?

Understanding computational complexity is crucial for writing efficient and scalable software. An algorithm that's fast on 100 items might be unusably slow on a million items. By analyzing the complexity, developers can:

- Choose the right algorithm for a given problem.
- Predict performance and identify potential bottlenecks before they happen.
- Design systems that can handle large amounts of data effectively.

The Model Selection Decision Framework

One of the easiest ways to spot a data scientist who has never had to carry a pager is to see how he/she chooses a model. The purely academic approach is a quest for the highest score on a leaderboard. It's a sprint to squeeze out another tenth of a percentage point of accuracy, often by reaching for the most complex, resource-hungry deep learning architecture imaginable. This is a recipe for production disaster.

In the world of deployed data science, it is not academics; We are engineers and architects. Our goal is not to build the most powerful theoretical engine. The goal is to build a reliable, efficient, and maintainable car that gets the business from point A to point B. Sometimes that requires a Formula 1 engine, but more often, it calls for a dependable V6. Choosing the right one is not a quest for the "best" model, but a strategic **trade-off analysis**.

To move from a purely accuracy-driven choice to a professional engineering decision, let's use a framework built on four pillars.

Pillar 1: Performance and Accuracy

Let's be clear: performance is the ticket to the game. If your model doesn't have sufficient predictive power, nothing else matters. But "accuracy" is a dangerously simplistic term. This pillar is about choosing the *right metric for the business problem.*

- **For a fraud detection system,** you are likely more concerned with **Recall** (catching as many fraudulent transactions as possible) than Precision, even if it means a few false positives for your review team. A missed fraud case costs real money.
- **For a spam filter,** you are obsessed with **Precision**. A false positive (flagging a legitimate email as spam) is a terrible user experience, far worse than letting one or two spam emails slip through to the inbox.
- **For an imbalanced classification problem** (like the churn model), a simple accuracy score is useless. A model that predicts "no churn" every time could have 99% accuracy but be completely worthless. Here, metrics like the **F1-Score** or **AUC-PR** (Area Under the Precision-Recall Curve) are far more informative.

Before you even compare models, you must have a clear, business-driven definition of what "good performance" means.

Pillar 2: Interpretability and Explainability (The "Why" Factor)

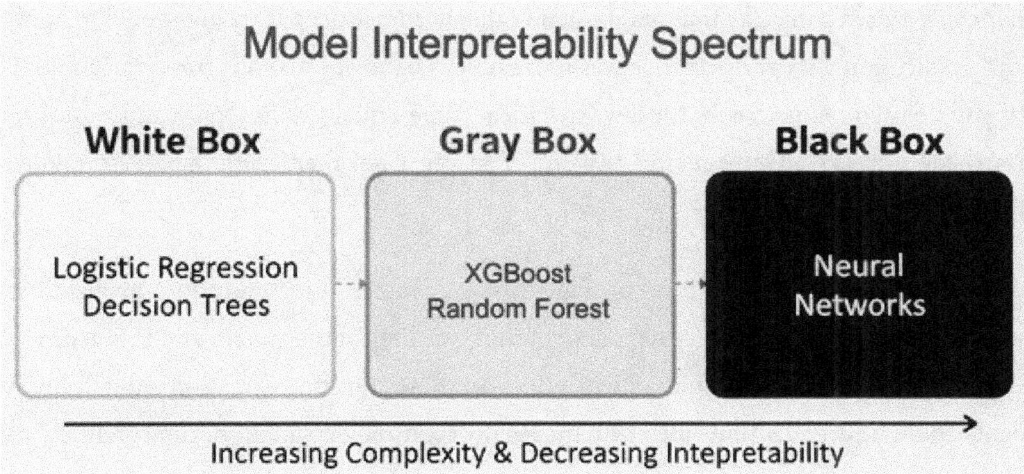

Figure 3.3. The spectrum of model interpretability, from transparent white boxes to opaque black boxes.

This is the pillar that is most often ignored in academia and most frequently demanded by the business. A model that produces a prediction without an explanation is a black box, and black boxes are a massive liability in the real world. Models exist on a spectrum of interpretability:

- **High Interpretability (White Box):** These are models whose inner workings are transparent by design. You can easily trace the path from input to output. Examples include **Linear/Logistic Regression** (where you can inspect the coefficients) and **Decision Trees** (where you can follow the branches).

- **Medium Interpretability (Gray Box):** This category includes ensemble models like **Random Forests** and **Gradient Boosting (XGBoost, LightGBM)**. You can get high-level explanations, such as feature importance charts, but explaining a single prediction is difficult.

- **Low Interpretability (Black Box):** This is the domain of **Deep Neural Networks** and Support Vector Machines (SVMs). They often provide the highest accuracy but are notoriously opaque. Understanding the decisions requires specialized, post-hoc **Explainable AI (XAI)** techniques like LIME or SHAP, which we will cover in a later chapter.

Field Story: The Loan Model vs. The Lawyers

At a financial services company that had built a highly accurate deep learning model to approve or deny loan applications. Its performance was incredible. There was just one problem. In the United States, if you deny someone credit, the law (specifically, the Equal Credit Opportunity Act) requires you to provide a clear "adverse action reason." You must tell them *why* they were denied (e.g., "insufficient credit history").

The team's black-box model could not provide this as a reason. It just outputs a probability score. The company's legal and compliance department took one look at the system and shut it down. They ended up deploying a much simpler, slightly less accurate logistic regression model, because its coefficients could be directly translated into the legally required explanation. Interpretability wasn't just a nice-to-have; it was a hard, legal requirement.

Pillar 3: Operational Efficiency (Cost and Speed)

This is where you put on your engineer's hat. A model doesn't just run once; it runs continuously, and that has a cost.

- **Training Cost and Time:** How long does it take to train the model, and on what hardware? A massive transformer model that takes three days to train on a cluster of 8 A100 GPUs might be acceptable for a research project. But if your business needs the model to be retrained daily on new data, it's operationally unfeasible.

- **Inference Latency (Speed):** How fast can the model make a single prediction? For a real-time fraud detection system, this is a non-negotiable requirement. A simple logistic regression might take ¡1 millisecond to run. A large XGBoost model might take 50 milliseconds. A large deep learning model could take 500 milliseconds or more. You must choose a model that meets the latency SLA of your product.

- **Model Footprint (Size):** How much memory and disk space does the model artifact occupy? A scikit-learn logistic regression model might be a few kilobytes. An XGBoost model could be tens of megabytes in size. A deep learning model can easily be several gigabytes. This is critically important for deploying models to the edge (e.g., on a mobile phone), but it also impacts the cost of your cloud servers.

Pillar 4: Maintainability and Simplicity

This is the most underrated pillar, but it is often the most important for a data product's long-term health. It's about choosing technology that your team can live with for years.

- **The "Boring Technology" Principle:** You should always, always start with the simplest, most "boring" model that could plausibly solve the problem (often a logistic regression or a simple decision tree). Only add complexity if you can prove, through experimentation, that a more complex model (like XGBoost) provides a significant and justifiable lift in business value. A simpler model is easier to debug, explain, deploy, and for new team members to understand and maintain.

- **Dependencies and Ecosystem:** Is the model built using a mainstream, well-supported library like Scikit-learn, XGBoost, TensorFlow, or PyTorch? Or is it using an obscure, experimental library from a PhD student's GitHub repo with no documentation and a bus factor of one? Choosing a mature ecosystem is a strategic decision that will save you countless hours of maintenance headaches down the road.

The Framework in Practice: A Decision Matrix

To make this process tangible, encourage teams to use a simple decision matrix. It turns a gut-feeling choice into a structured, defensible analysis. You list your candidate models and score them against the key criteria, weighting them by the criteria that matter most to your specific project.

Model	Performance (Weight:40)	Interpretability (Weight: 30%)	Op. Efficiency (Weight:20%)	Maintainability (Weight: 10%)
Logistic Regression	3	5	5	5
XGBoost	5	3	3	4
Neural Network	5	1	2	3

Table 3.2. Example Model Selection Decision Matrix (1=Worst, 5=Best).

In this hypothetical scenario for the loan denial model, even though XGBoost and the Neural Network achieve the highest performance, the weighted score might favor the simpler Logistic Regression due to the strong business requirement for interpretability. This matrix makes that trade-off explicit and easy to communicate to stakeholders.

The deployed data scientist is an architect who chooses the right tool for the job, not a researcher who always builds the most complex machine possible. This framework is your guide to making that professional choice.

Moving beyond basic accuracy requires sophisticated evaluation frameworks that align with business objectives and account for real-world constraints.

Advanced Evaluation Metrics

A single accuracy score is a fool's errand. In the real world, where business problems are messy and imbalanced, relying on a single accuracy number is one of the fastest ways to deploy a model that is useless or, even worse, actively harmful. Think of it this way: you wouldn't judge a car's performance solely on its top speed. You care about its acceleration, handling, fuel efficiency, and safety rating. A model is no different. To truly understand its performance, you need a diagnostic dashboard, not just a single number. This section is your guide to building that dashboard.

The Imbalance Problem: Precision, Recall, and the F1- Score

The first and most critical lesson is that most interesting business problems involve heavily imbalanced classes.

- **Fraud Detection:** 99.9% of transactions are legitimate.
- **Predictive Maintenance:** 99% of machine parts are not about to fail.
- **Customer Churn:** 95% of your customers are happy and will not leave this month.

In these scenarios, a naive model that always predicts the majority class (e.g., "not fraud") will have sky-high accuracy (99.9%) while being completely useless. To get a true picture, we must look inside the predictions using a Confusion Matrix.

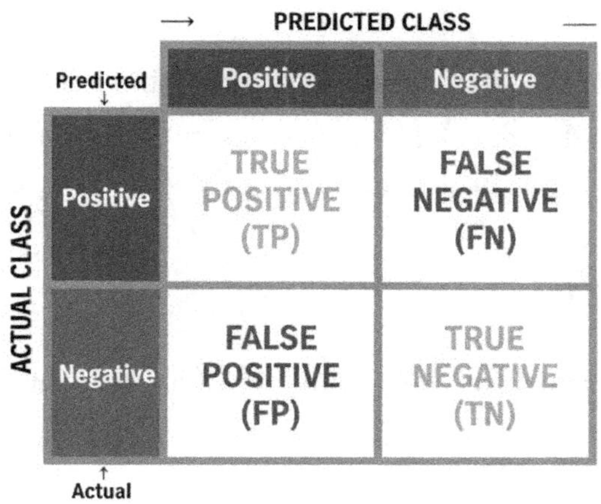

Figure 3.4. The Confusion Matrix: The source of truth for classification metrics.

The matrix gives us the four possible outcomes of a prediction:

- **True Positive (TP):** The model correctly predicted 'fraud'. You caught a criminal.
- **False Positive (FP):** The model incorrectly predicted 'fraud'. You blocked a good customer's transaction (a Type I error).
- **True Negative (TN):** The model correctly predicted 'not fraud'. A legitimate transaction went through smoothly.
- **False Negative (FN):** The model incorrectly predicted 'not fraud'. A fraudulent transaction was approved (a Type II error).

From these four numbers, we can derive the metrics that truly matter.

Precision: The Certainty Metric

The Question: Of all the times the model sounded the alarm (predicted positive), how often was it **right**?

$$Precision = \frac{TP}{TP + FP}$$

The Business Implication: High precision minimizes false positives. You use this when the cost of a false positive is high.

Use Case: Spam Filtering. You would rather let one spam email slip into the inbox (a false negative) than send a critical job offer to the spam folder (a false positive). Your goal is to be very certain that when you flag an email as spam, it really is spam.

Recall: The Completeness Metric

The Question: Of all the actual positive cases in the world, what fraction did the model successfully catch?

$$Recall = \frac{TP}{TP + FN}$$

The Business Implication: High recall minimizes false negatives. You use this when the cost of a false negative is high.

Use Case: Medical Diagnosis. For a cancer screening model, you absolutely want to catch every possible case. A false positive (flagging a healthy patient for more tests) is an inconvenience, but a false negative (missing a real case) can be fatal.

The Precision-Recall Trade-off and the F1-Score

Precision and recall are almost always in tension. If you tune your model to be more sensitive to catch more fraud (increasing recall), you will inevitably flag more legitimate transactions as well (decreasing precision). The choice of which to prioritize is a business decision, not a data science one. When you need a single metric that balances both, you use the **F1-Score**. It is the harmonic mean of precision and recall.

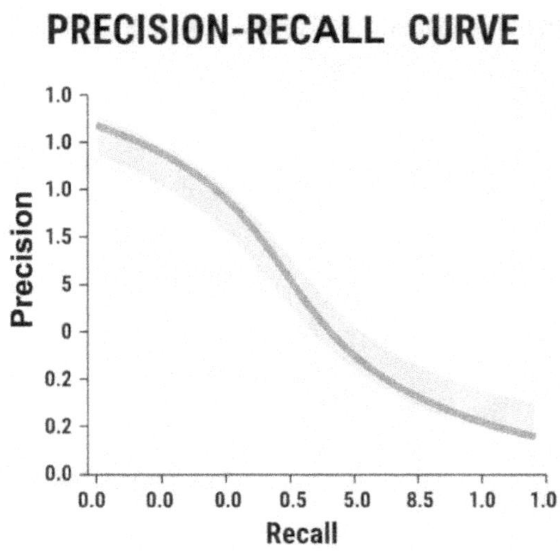

Figure 3.5. The classic trade-off: increasing recall often comes at the cost of precision.

$$\text{F1} - \text{Score} = 2\,\text{X}\frac{\text{Precision} \times \text{Recall}}{\text{Precision} + \text{Recall}}$$

The F1-Score is particularly useful when you have imbalanced classes, as it provides a more realistic measure of a model's performance than accuracy.

Beyond a Single Threshold: ROC-AUC

Most classification models don't just output a binary prediction; they output a probability score (e.g., this transaction has an 85% probability of being fraudulent). To turn this into a 'fraud'/'not fraud' decision, you apply a threshold (e.g., if probability > 0.5, predict 'fraud'). But is 0.5 the right threshold? If you lower it to 0.3, you'll increase your recall (catching more fraud) but lower your precision (falser positives). How can you evaluate the model's overall quality, independent of any single threshold? The answer is the **ROC Curve** and its corresponding metric, **AUC**.

ROC Curve (Receiver Operating Characteristic): This curve plots the **True Positive Rate** (which is just another name for Recall) against the **False Positive Rate** across all possible thresholds. A model that is no better than a random guess will have a straight diagonal line. A good model will have a curve that bows up towards the top-left corner.

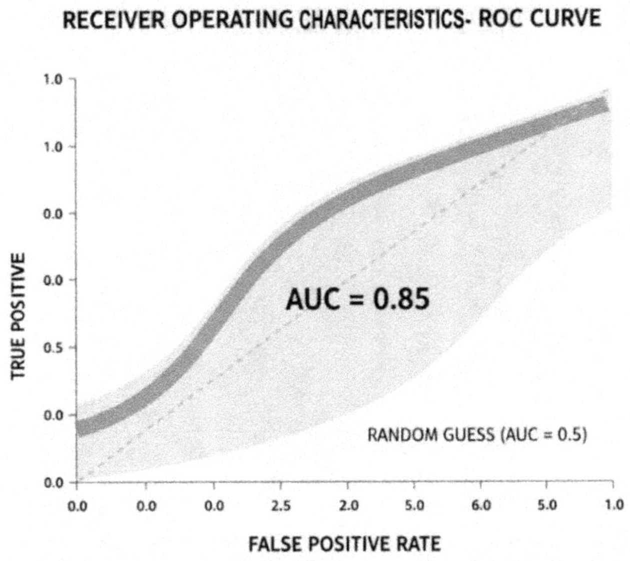

Figure 3.6. An ROC curve, with the Area Under the Curve (AUC) representing the model's overall performance.

AUC (Area Under the Curve): This is a single number, from 0 to 1, that summarizes the entire ROC curve. Its intuitive meaning is powerful: **AUC represents the probability that the model will rank a randomly chosen positive instance higher than a randomly chosen negative instance.** An AUC of 0.5 is a random guess. An AUC of 1.0 is a perfect classifier. ROC-AUC is one of the best general-purpose metrics for evaluating a classifier's overall predictive power.

For Probabilistic Predictions: Log-Loss

Sometimes you don't just care about the final classification; you care about the model's confidence. A model that correctly predicts "fraud" with 99% confidence is much better than one that predicts it with a shaky 51% confidence.

Logarithmic Loss (Log-Loss) is the best metric for evaluating the quality of a model's *probabilistic* predictions. It heavily penalizes a model for being both confident and wrong. A model that predicts a 99% probability of "not fraud" for a transaction that was fraudulent will get a huge penalty. A less confident model (e.g., predicted 60% "not fraud") will get a smaller penalty. Your goal is to minimize the log-loss. You should use log-loss when the actual probability outputs are important; for example, when a model's output is used for risk assessment, insurance pricing, or as an input feature to another downstream system. We, the deployed data scientists, don't rely on a single metric. We build a comprehensive diagnostic dashboard using a suite of metrics that are aligned with the specific business problem. This is how you move from a vanity score to a true understanding of your model's behavior.

```
from scipy import stats
from sklearn.metrics import accuracy_score, f1_score
import numpy as np
class StatisticalModelEvaluator:
    """Statistical testing for model comparison and validation"""
    def mcnemar_test(self, y_true, y_pred1, y_pred2, alpha=0.05):
        """McNemar's test for paired binary classifiers"""
        # Create contingency table
        both_correct = np.sum((y_pred1 == y_true) & (y_pred2 == y_true))
        both_wrong = np.sum((y_pred1 != y_true) & (y_pred2 != y_true))
        first_correct = np.sum((y_pred1 == y_true) & (y_pred2 != y_true))
        second_correct = np.sum((y_pred1 != y_true) & (y_pred2 == y_true))
        # Calculate test statistic
        b = first_correct
        c = second_correct
        if b + c < 25:  # Use exact binomial test for small samples
            p_value = stats.binom_test(min(b, c), b + c, 0.5)
        else:  # Use chi-square approximation
            chi2 = (abs(b - c) - 1) ** 2 / (b + c)
            p_value = 1 - stats.chi2.cdf(chi2, 1)
        significant = p_value < alpha
        return {
            'p_value': p_value,
            'significant': significant,
            'test_statistic': abs(b - c),
            'contingency_table': {
                'both_correct': both_correct,
                'both_wrong': both_wrong,
                'only_first_correct': first_correct,
                'only_second_correct': second_correct
            }
        }
    def paired_t_test(self, model1_scores, model2_scores, alpha=0.05):
        """Paired t-test for model performance scores"""
        differences = [s1 - s2 for s1, s2 in zip(model1_scores, model2_scores)]
        t_stat, p_value = stats.ttest_rel(model1_scores, model2_scores)
        significant = p_value < alpha
        effect_size = np.mean(differences) / np.std(differences)
        return {
            't_statistic': t_stat,
            'p_value': p_value,
            'significant': significant,
            'effect_size': effect_size,
            'mean_difference': np.mean(differences)
        }
    def confidence_intervals(self, scores, confidence=0.95):
        """Calculate confidence intervals for performance metrics"""
        n = len(scores)
        mean = np.mean(scores)
        std_err = stats.sem(scores)
        # Calculate confidence interval
        h = std_err * stats.t.ppf((1 + confidence) / 2, n - 1)
        return {
            'mean': mean,
            'std_error': std_err,
            'confidence_interval': (mean - h, mean + h),
            'margin_of_error': h
        }
# Bayesian evaluation methods
class BayesianModelEvaluator:
    """Bayesian methods for model evaluation with uncertainty quantification"""
    def bayesian_correlation(self, x, y, n_samples=10000):
        """Bayesian correlation analysis"""
        # Using Bayesian approach to estimate correlation with uncertainty
        import pymc3 as pm
        with pm.Model() as model:
            # Priors
            mu_x = pm.Normal('mu_x', mu=np.mean(x), sigma=10)
            mu_y = pm.Normal('mu_y', mu=np.mean(y), sigma=10)
            sigma_x = pm.HalfNormal('sigma_x', sigma=10)
            sigma_y = pm.HalfNormal('sigma_y', sigma=10)
            rho = pm.Uniform('rho', lower=-1, upper=1)
            # Covariance matrix
            cov = pm.Deterministic('cov', tt.stacklists([
                [sigma_x ** 2, sigma_x * sigma_y * rho],
                [sigma_x * sigma_y * rho, sigma_y ** 2]
            ]))
            # Likelihood
            obs = pm.MvNormal('obs', mu=[mu_x, mu_y], cov=cov, observed=[x, y])
            # Sample
            trace = pm.sample(n_samples, tune=1000, return_inferencedata=False)
        return trace
```

Listing 3.2: Statistical testing for model comparison and validation.

Cost-Sensitive Learning and Business Metric Translation

```
import numpy as np_
from sklearn.utils import class_weight
from sklearn.metrics import precision_score, recall_score, f1_score
import pandas as pd
from typing import Dict
class BusinessMetricTranslator:
    """Translate technical metrics to business impact"""
    def __init__(self, cost_matrix: Dict, business_parameters: Dict):
        """Initialize with cost matrix and business parameters.
        Args:
            cost_matrix: Dictionary with costs for TP, FP, TN, FN
            business_parameters: Business-specific parameters
        """
        self.cost_matrix = cost_matrix
        self.business_params = business_parameters
    def _confusion_matrix(self, y_true, y_pred):
        """Calculate confusion matrix components"""
        tp = np.sum((y_true == 1) & (y_pred == 1))
        fp = np.sum((y_true == 0) & (y_pred == 1))
        tn = np.sum((y_true == 0) & (y_pred == 0))
        fn = np.sum((y_true == 1) & (y_pred == 0))
        return {'tp': tp, 'fp': fp, 'tn': tn, 'fn': fn}
    def calculate_business_value(self, y_true, y_pred, y_pred_proba=None):
        """Calculate actual business value of predictions"""
        cm = self._confusion_matrix(y_true, y_pred)
        # Calculate costs and benefits
        total_cost = (
            cm['tp'] * self.cost_matrix.get('tp_cost', 0) +
            cm['fp'] * self.cost_matrix.get('fp_cost', 0) +
            cm['tn'] * self.cost_matrix.get('tn_cost', 0) +
            cm['fn'] * self.cost_matrix.get('fn_cost', 0)
        )
        total_revenue = (
            cm['tp'] * self.cost_matrix.get('tp_revenue', 0) +
            cm['tn'] * self.cost_matrix.get('tn_revenue', 0)
        )
        net_value = total_revenue - total_cost
        return {
            'confusion_matrix': cm,
            'total_cost': total_cost,
            'total_revenue': total_revenue,
            'net_value': net_value,
            'roi': net_value / abs(total_cost) if total_cost != 0 else float('inf')
        }
    def find_optimal_threshold(self, y_true, y_pred_proba):
        """Find threshold that maximizes business value"""
        thresholds = np.linspace(0, 1, 100)
        business_values = []
        for threshold in thresholds:
            y_pred = (y_pred_proba >= threshold).astype(int)
            business_value = self.calculate_business_value(y_true, y_pred)
            business_values.append(business_value['net_value'])
        optimal_idx = np.argmax(business_values)
```

```
        max_value = business_values[optimal_idx]
        return optimal_threshold, max_value
    def expected_value_frame(self, y_true, y_pred_proba):
        """Create expected value framework for decision making"""
        thresholds = np.linspace(0, 1, 50)
        results = []
        for threshold in thresholds:
            y_pred = (y_pred_proba >= threshold).astype(int)
            business_result = self.calculate_business_value(y_true, y_pred)
            results.append({
                'threshold': threshold,
                'net_value': business_result['net_value'],
                'precision': precision_score(y_true, y_pred, zero_division=0),
                'recall': recall_score(y_true, y_pred),
                'f1': f1_score(y_true, y_pred)
            })
        return pd.DataFrame(results)
class CostSensitiveClassifier:
    """Implement cost-sensitive learning techniques"""
    def __init__(self, base_estimator, cost_matrix):
        self.base_estimator = base_estimator
        self.cost_matrix = cost_matrix
    def fit(self, X, y, sample_weights=None):
        """Fit model with cost-sensitive adjustments"""
        if sample_weights is None:
            # Calculate weights based on cost matrix
            sample_weights = self._calculate_cost_weights(y)
        return self.base_estimator.fit(X, y, sample_weight=sample_weights)
    def _calculate_cost_weights(self, y):
        """Calculate sample weights based on misclassification costs"""
        weights = np.ones(len(y))
        # Example: Higher weight for minority class if misclassification is costly
        class_weights = class_weight.compute_class_weight(
            'balanced', classes=np.unique(y), y=y
        )
        # Adjust weights based on cost matrix
        for i, (class_val, weight) in enumerate(zip(np.unique(y), class_weights)):
            # Incorporate business costs into weights
            cost_adjustment = self._get_class_cost(class_val)
            weights[y == class_val] = weight * cost_adjustment
        return weights
    def _get_class_cost(self, class_val):
        """Get misclassification cost for a class"""
        # Implementation depends on specific cost matrix structure
        return 1.0  # Default implementation_
```

Listing 3.3: Business-aligned model evaluation and cost-sensitive learning.

The Model Registry: Your Single Source of Truth

A robust model registry is the cornerstone of MLOps, providing version control, lineage tracking, and governance for machine learning models. Let's be honest. If you've ever worked on a data science project for more than a few weeks, your project folder has probably looked something like this:

- Churn model final.pkl
- churn model final v2.pkl
- churn model final v2 with new features.pkl
- churn model final v2 REALLY FINAL this time.pkl

We've all been there. It's the artisanal, craft-based approach to model management. It's a system that relies on file names and human memory to keep track of its most important assets. And it is a recipe for absolute chaos in a production environment.

What data was used to train 'v2'? What was the AUC score for the "new features" version? Which exact version is currently running in production and making decisions that impact the business? In this file-based world, these critical questions are often impossible to answer.

This is the problem that a **Model Registry** solves. It is the cornerstone of any mature MLOps practice. A model registry is a centralized system for managing the entire lifecycle of a machine learning model, from experiment to production to retirement. It is to models what Git and GitHub are to code: a versioned, collaborative, and auditable single source of truth.

Why a Registry? Beyond a Pickled File

Moving from a folder of '.pkl' files to a model registry is a fundamental shift from a chaotic craft to a disciplined engineering practice. The "why" comes down to three core pillars:

- **Reproducibility:** This is the bedrock of all science and engineering. If a customer or an auditor asks why your model made a specific prediction six months ago, you must be able to answer. Without a registry, this is impossible. You'd have to find the old model file, guess which version of the code was used to serve it, and hope you can find the exact data that went into it. A model registry solves this by creating an immutable link between a model version, the code that produced it, and the data it was trained on.

- **Collaboration:** A model is rarely the work of a single person. How does a team collaborate on improving a model? How does a new team member get up to speed on the history of experiments that led to the current production version? The registry provides a central, shared repository for all experiments and production-ready models, acting as a living document of the team's collective work.

- **Audit and Compliance:** In many industries, especially finance and healthcare, you are legally required to have a clear, auditable trail for your models. You must be able to prove to regulators which model version was active at a specific time, how it was validated, and when it was approved for production. A model registry is the system of record that enables this.

Key Features of a Modern Model Registry

While specific tools vary, any robust model registry provides a core set of features that work together to manage a model's lifecycle.

Model Versioning

This is the most fundamental feature. Every time a new model is trained and registered, it is assigned a unique, immutable version (e.g., 'churn-predictor:v12'). This eliminates the 'final v2' chaos and provides a clear, unambiguous way to reference a specific model artifact.

Experiment Tracking

A model registry is almost always linked to an experiment tracking system. Every training run is logged as an "experiment," capturing all the critical metadata needed for reproducibility:

- **Hyperparameters:** The settings used for the training run (e.g., learning rate, tree depth).

- **Evaluation Metrics:** The performance of the model on a validation set (e.g., AUC, F1-Score, Log-Loss).
- **Data Pointers:** The version or location of the training and validation datasets.
- **Code Version:** The Git commit hash of the code that ran the training.

Model Lineage

This is where the true power of a registry becomes clear. It connects all the dots from experiment tracking to provide a complete lineage graph for every model. For any given model in production, the registry can answer the question: "Where did this come from?"

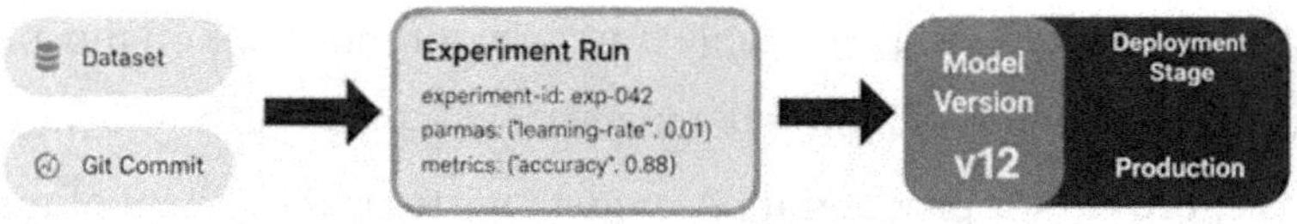

Figure 3.6. A model lineage graph, providing a complete, auditable trail from data to deployment.

The lineage trail looks like this: This production model 'v12' came from experiment run 'exp-042', which was trained on code from Git commit 'f00bar', using the dataset 'customers 2025-09.parquet'.

Model Staging and Governance

A model doesn't just go from "trained" to "production." The registry manages the promotion of a model through a series of stages, providing a crucial governance layer. A typical workflow looks like:

1. A data scientist registers a new model version. It automatically starts in the **Staging** stage.
2. The MLOps pipeline runs a suite of automated validation tests against the staging model.
3. If the tests pass, a senior team member or manager receives a notification to review the model's performance and can approve its promotion to **Production**.
4. The CI/CD system sees that a new model has been promoted to Production and automatically deploys it.
5. An older model might be moved to the **Archived** stage.

This workflow prevents developers from accidentally pushing an unvalidated model to production and establishes a clear, human-in-the-loop approval gate.

The Model Registry in Practice

Open-Source Example: MLflow

MLflow is one of the most popular open-source platforms for managing the ML lifecycle, and its Model Registry is excellent. Here is a simple Python snippet that shows how to use MLflow to track an experiment and register the resulting model.

```
import mlflow
import mlflow.sklearn
from sklearn.ensemble import RandomForestClassifier
from sklearn.metrics import accuracy_score
from sklearn.datasets import load_breast_cancer
from sklearn.model_selection import train_test_split
# Load sample data
data = load_breast_cancer()
X, y = data.data, data.target
X_train, X_val, y_train, y_val = train_test_split(X, y, test_size=0.2, random_state=42)
# MLflow automatically logs to a local file or a remote server
mlflow.set_experiment("Churn Prediction")
with mlflow.start_run() as run:
    # 1. Log Hyperparameters
    n_estimators = 100
    max_depth = 10
    mlflow.log_param("n_estimators", n_estimators)
    mlflow.log_param("max_depth", max_depth)
    # Train the model
    model = RandomForestClassifier(n_estimators=n_estimators, max_depth=max_depth)
    model.fit(X_train, y_train)
    # 2. Log Evaluation Metrics
    predictions = model.predict(X_val)
    accuracy = accuracy_score(y_val, predictions)
    mlflow.log_metric("validation_accuracy", accuracy)
    # 3. Log the model and register it
    # This versions the model and places it in the registry
    mlflow.sklearn.log_model(
        sk_model=model, artifact_path="churn-model", registered_model_name="churn-predictor"
    )
print(f"Run ID: {run.info.run_id}")
```

Listing 3.4: A Python code block.

After running this code, you could go to the MLflow UI, see your experiment, and find the new version of the "churn-predictor" model in the registry, ready to be moved from 'Staging' to 'Production'.

Cloud-Native Registries

All major cloud providers offer tightly integrated model registries as part of their MLOps platforms.

- **AWS SageMaker Model Registry:** Part of the Amazon SageMaker ecosystem, it integrates seamlessly with SageMaker Pipelines for automated training, registration, and deployment.
- **Google Cloud Vertex AI Model Registry:** A central component of the unified Vertex AI platform, allowing you to manage models for both batch and online prediction.
- **Azure Machine Learning Model Registry:** Integrated into the Azure ML workspace, it provides versioning, lineage, and deployment management for models trained in Azure.

While the specific APIs and UIs differ, the core concepts: versioning, lineage, and staging are universal.

A model registry is the system that transforms your model development from a chaotic, file-based craft into a disciplined, reproducible engineering practice. It is the single source of truth that allows a deployed data scientist to sleep at night.

Advanced Model Registry Implementation

```
from datetime import datetime
from enum import Enum
from typing import Dict, List, Optional
import logging
import mlflow
import numpy as np
from mlflow.entities.model_registry import ModelVersion
class ModelStage(Enum):
    NONE = "None"
    STAGING = "Staging"
    PRODUCTION = "Production"
    ARCHIVED = "Archived"
class ModelRegistryManager:
    """Advanced model registry with governance and lifecycle management"""
    def __init__(self, tracking_uri: str, registry_uri: str):
        mlflow.set_tracking_uri(tracking_uri)
        mlflow.set_registry_uri(registry_uri)
        self.client = mlflow.tracking.MlflowClient()
    def register_model(self, model, run_id: str, model_name: str,
                       model_signature, metadata: Dict) -> ModelVersion:
        """Register model with comprehensive metadata"""
        # Validate model signature
        if not self._validate_signature(model_signature):
            raise ValueError("Invalid model signature")
        with mlflow.start_run(run_id=run_id):
            # Log model with signature
            mlflow.sklearn.log_model(
                model,
                "model", signature=model_signature, registered_model_name=model_name, metadata=metadata)
            # Get the registered model
            model_uri = f"runs:/{run_id}/model"
            registered_model = mlflow.register_model(model_uri, model_name)
            # Add version-specific metadata
            self.client.set_model_version_tag(
                model_name, registered_model.version,
                "registered_timestamp", datetime.now().isoformat())
            return registered_model
    def promote_model(self, model_name: str, version: int,
                      target_stage: ModelStage, approval_required: bool = True) -> bool:
        """Promote model to target stage with approval workflow"""
        if approval_required and not self._get_approval(model_name, version, target_stage):
            logging.warning(f"Approval denied for {model_name} version {version}")
            return False
        # Check promotion criteria
        if not self._meets_promotion_criteria(model_name, version, target_stage):
            logging.error(f"Promotion criteria not met for {model_name} version {version}")
        # Transition stage
        self.client.transition_model_version_stage(
            name=model_name, version=version,
            stage=target_stage.value)
        # Archive previous versions if promoting to production
        if target_stage == ModelStage.PRODUCTION:
            self._archive_previous_versions(model_name, version)
```

```
        logging.info(f"Successfully promoted {model_name} version {version} to {target_stage.value}")
        return True
    def _validate_signature(self, signature) -> bool:
        """Validate model input/output signature"""
        try:
            # Check signature structure and types
            required_fields = ['inputs', 'outputs']
            if not all(field in signature for field in required_fields):
                return False
            # Validate input schema
            for input_spec in signature['inputs']:
                if not all(k in input_spec for k in ['name', 'type', 'required']):
                    return False
            return True
        except:
            return False
    def _meets_promotion_criteria(self, model_name: str, version: int,
                                  target_stage: ModelStage) -> bool:
        """Check if model meets promotion criteria for target stage"""
        model_version = self.client.get_model_version(model_name, version)
        criteria = {
            ModelStage.STAGING: self._staging_criteria,
            ModelStage.PRODUCTION: self._production_criteria,
            ModelStage.ARCHIVED: self._archival_criteria}
        criteria_func = criteria.get(target_stage)
        return criteria_func(model_version) if criteria_func else True
    def _production_criteria(self, model_version) -> bool:
        """Criteria for promoting to production"""
        # Performance thresholds
        run = self.client.get_run(model_version.run_id)
        metrics = run.data.metrics
        required_metrics = {
            'validation_accuracy': 0.85,
            'validation_precision': 0.80,
            'validation_recall': 0.75,
            'validation_f1': 0.78}
        for metric, threshold in required_metrics.items():
            if metrics.get(metric, 0) < threshold:
                return False
        # Business validation
        business_metric = metrics.get('business_value', 0)
        if business_metric <= 0:
            return False
        # Stability checks
        cv_scores = metrics.get('cv_scores', [])
        if cv_scores and np.std(cv_scores) > 0.05:  # High variance
            return False
        return True
    def create_model_card(self, model_name: str, version: int) -> Dict:
        """Generate comprehensive model card"""
        model_version = self.client.get_model_version(model_name, version)
```

```
        model_version = self.client.get_model_version(model_name, version)
        run = self.client.get_run(model_version.run_id)
        return {
            'model_details': {
                'name': model_name,
                'version': version,
                'stage': model_version.current_stage,
                'description': run.data.tags.get('description', ''),
                'registered_date': model_version.creation_timestamp},
            'performance_metrics': run.data.metrics,
            'hyperparameters': run.data.params,
            'data_sources': self._get_data_lineage(run),
            'ethical_considerations': self._get_ethical_info(run),
            'limitations': run.data.tags.get('limitations', ''),
            'usage_instructions': run.data.tags.get('usage_instructions', '')}
# Model lineage and dependency tracking
class ModelLineageTracker:
    """Track model dependencies and lineage"""
    def __init__(self, registry_manager: ModelRegistryManager):
        self.registry = registry_manager
    def track_dependencies(self, model_name: str, version: int) -> Dict:
        """Track all dependencies for a model version"""
        model_version = self.registry.client.get_model_version(model_name, version)
        run = self.registry.client.get_run(model_version.run_id)
        dependencies = {
            'data_dependencies': self._extract_data_dependencies(run),
            'code_dependencies': self._extract_code_dependencies(run),
            'model_dependencies': self._extract_model_dependencies(run),
            'infrastructure_dependencies': self._extract_infrastructure_dependencies(run)}
        return dependencies
    def _extract_data_dependencies(self, run) -> List[Dict]:
        """Extract data dependencies from run artifacts"""
        data_deps = []
        # Check for data version tags
        data_version = run.data.tags.get('data_version')
        if data_version:
            data_deps.append({
                'type': 'training_data',
                'version': data_version,
                'source': run.data.tags.get('data_source', 'unknown')})
        # Check for feature store references
        feature_store_ref = run.data.tags.get('feature_store_version')
        if feature_store_ref:
            data_deps.append({
                'type': 'feature_store',
                'version': feature_store_ref})
        return data_deps
```

Listing 3.5: Production-ready model registry.

Feature Engineering Pipeline

Professional feature engineering goes beyond basic transformations to include automation, monitoring, and versioning. A **feature engineering pipeline** is an automated system that transforms raw data into clean, informative features that enable a machine learning model to make accurate predictions. Instead of performing these steps manually in a notebook, a pipeline is a series of repeatable, version-controlled code that ensures consistency between model training and live inference. It is a cornerstone of MLOps, bridging the gap between raw data and a production-ready model.

Key Stages of a Feature Engineering Pipeline

Data Ingestion and Splitting: The pipeline begins by loading the raw data. The first critical step is splitting it into training, validation, and test sets to prevent data leakage, where information from the test set inadvertently influences the training process.

Data Cleaning and Imputation: This stage addresses data errors and missing values. Common steps include:

- **Handling Missing Values:** Imputing (filling in) missing data using strategies like the mean, median, or a constant value.
- **Correcting Data Types:** Ensuring numerical columns are treated as numbers and categorical columns as objects or strings.
- **Outlier Removal:** Identifying and removing extreme data points that could negatively skew the model.

Feature Transformation: This involves modifying existing features to suit the model better.

- **Numerical Features:** Techniques such as **scaling** (e.g., StandardScaler or MinMaxScaler) normalize feature ranges, which is crucial for many algorithms.
- **Categorical Features:** Converting non-numeric data into a numeric format using methods like **one-hot encoding** (creating binary columns for each category) or **label encoding** (assigning a unique integer to each category).

- **Feature Creation:** This is often the most creative step, where new features are engineered from existing ones based on domain knowledge.
- **From Timestamps:** Extracting features like day of week, month, or whether it is a weekend.
- **From Text:** Creating numerical features using techniques like TF-IDF or word embeddings.
- **Aggregations:** Creating features like a customer's average purchase amount or number of transactions.
- **Feature Selection:** After creating many potential features, this final step often involves selecting only the most predictive ones to reduce model complexity, decrease training time, and prevent overfitting.

Why It's a "Pipeline"

Automating these steps into a pipeline is critical for production ML. It ensures the same transformations are applied to both the historical data used for training and the new, live data used for predictions. This consistency prevents **training-serving skew**, a common and subtle cause of model failure in production.

Automated Feature Engineering

```
import pandas as pd
import numpy as np
from typing import Dict, List
from sklearn.base import BaseEstimator, TransformerMixin
from sklearn.pipeline import Pipeline
from datetime import datetime
class AutomatedFeatureEngineer(BaseEstimator, TransformerMixin):
    """Automated feature engineering with multiple techniques"""
    def __init__(self, feature_config: Dict):
        self.feature_config = feature_config
        self.feature_names_ = []
    def fit(self, X, y=None):
        """Learn feature engineering parameters"""
        self.feature_names_ = list(X.columns)
        # Learn statistical properties for normalization
        if self.feature_config.get('normalize', False):
            self.means_ = X.mean()
            self.stds_ = X.std()
        # Learn categorical encodings
        if self.feature_config.get('encode_categoricals', False):
            self.category_mappings_ = {}
            for col in X.select_dtypes(include=['object']).columns:
                self.category_mappings_[col] = X[col].value_counts().to_dict()
        return self
    def transform(self, X):
        """Apply feature engineering transformations"""
        X_transformed = X.copy()
        # Handle missing values
        if self.feature_config.get('handle_missing', True):
            X_transformed = self._handle_missing_values(X_transformed)
        # Create interaction features
        if self.feature_config.get('interactions', False):
            X_transformed = self._create_interactions(X_transformed)
        # Create polynomial features
        if self.feature_config.get('polynomials', False):
            X_transformed = self._create_polynomials(X_transformed)
        # Create temporal features
        if self.feature_config.get('temporal_features', False):
            X_transformed = self._create_temporal_features(X_transformed)
        # Apply normalization
        if self.feature_config.get('normalize', False):
            X_transformed = self._normalize_features(X_transformed)
        # Update feature names
        self.feature_names_ = list(X_transformed.columns)
        return X_transformed
    def _handle_missing_values(self, X):
        """Automated missing value handling"""
        for col in X.columns:
            if X[col].isnull().sum() > 0:
                if X[col].dtype in ['float64', 'int64']:
                    # Numerical: impute with median
                    X[col].fillna(X[col].median(), inplace=True)
                else:
```

```
                X[col].fillna(X[col].median(), inplace=True)
            else:
                # Categorical: impute with mode
                X[col].fillna(X[col].mode()[0] if not X[col].mode().empty else 'missing', inplace=True)
        return X
    def _create_interactions(self, X):
        """Create interaction features between important variables"""
        numerical_cols = X.select_dtypes(include=[np.number]).columns
        # Create interactions for top correlated pairs
        if len(numerical_cols) >= 2:
            # Simple implementation: create interactions for first few columns
            for i, col1 in enumerate(numerical_cols[:3]):
                for col2 in numerical_cols[i+1:4]:
                    X[f'{col1}_x_{col2}'] = X[col1] * X[col2]
        return X
class FeatureStoreManager:
    """Manage feature storage and versioning"""
    def __init__(self, store_type: str = "offline"):
        self.store_type = store_type
        self.feature_versions = {}
    def store_features(self, features: pd.DataFrame,
                      feature_set_name: str,
                      version: str,
                      metadata: Dict):
        """Store features with versioning"""
        # Store to appropriate backend (database, data lake, etc.)
        storage_key = f"{feature_set_name}_{version}"
        # Store features
        self._store_to_backend(features, storage_key)
        # Store metadata
        self.feature_versions[storage_key] = {
            'metadata': metadata,
            'created_at': datetime.now(),
            'feature_count': features.shape[1],
            'row_count': features.shape[0]
        }
    def retrieve_features(self, feature_set_name: str, version: str,
                         entity_ids: List = None) -> pd.DataFrame:
        """Retrieve specific feature version"""
        storage_key = f"{feature_set_name}_{version}"
        if storage_key not in self.feature_versions:
            raise ValueError(f"Feature set {feature_set_name} version {version} not found")
        features = self._retrieve_from_backend(storage_key)
        if entity_ids:
            # Filter for specific entities
            index_col = self.feature_versions[storage_key]['metadata'].get('index_column')
            if index_col and index_col in features.columns:
                features = features[features[index_col].isin(entity_ids)]
        return features
    def _store_to_backend(self, features, storage_key):
        """Placeholder for storing features to backend"""
        pass
    def _retrieve_from_backend(self, storage_key):
```

```
        ‹pass
    def _retrieve_from_backend(self, storage_key):
        """Placeholder for retrieving features from backend"""
        pass
# Feature monitoring and validation
class FeatureMonitor:
    """Monitor feature quality and drift over time"""
    def __init__(self, reference_features: pd.DataFrame):
        self.reference_stats = self._calculate_feature_stats(reference_features)
    def monitor_drift(self, current_features: pd.DataFrame) -> Dict:
        """Monitor feature drift compared to reference"""
        current_stats = self._calculate_feature_stats(current_features)
        drift_report = {}
        for feature in self.reference_stats.keys():
            if feature in current_stats:
                ref_stats = self.reference_stats[feature]
                curr_stats = current_stats[feature]
                # Calculate drift metrics
                numerical_drift = self._calculate_numerical_drift(ref_stats, curr_stats)
                categorical_drift = self._calculate_categorical_drift(ref_stats, curr_stats)
                drift_report[feature] = {
                    'numerical_drift': numerical_drift,
                    'categorical_drift': categorical_drift,
                    'drift_detected': numerical_drift > 0.1 or categorical_drift > 0.1
                }
        return drift_report
    def _calculate_numerical_drift(self, ref_stats: Dict, curr_stats: Dict) -> float:
        """Calculate drift for numerical features"""
        if 'mean' not in ref_stats:
            return 0.0
        mean_drift = abs(ref_stats['mean'] - curr_stats['mean']) / (ref_stats['std'] + 1e-8)
        std_drift = abs(ref_stats['std'] - curr_stats['std']) / (ref_stats['std'] + 1e-8)
        return max(mean_drift, std_drift)
    def _calculate_feature_stats(self, features: pd.DataFrame) -> Dict:
        """Calculate statistics for features"""
        stats = {}
        for col in features.select_dtypes(include=[np.number]).columns:
            stats[col] = {
                'mean': features[col].mean(),
                'std': features[col].std(),
                'min': features[col].min(),
                'max': features[col].max()
            }
        return stats
    def _calculate_categorical_drift(self, ref_stats: Dict, curr_stats: Dict) -> float:
        """Calculate drift for categorical features"""
        return 0.0
```

Listing 3.6: Automated feature engineering pipeline.

Model Interpretability and Explainability

Building transparent models is crucial for trust, compliance, and debugging. Imagine you discover a brilliant doctor. They have an almost supernatural ability to diagnose complex diseases, with a success rate far exceeding that of any other physician. There's just one catch: when you ask them *how* they reached a diagnosis, they can't tell you. They say, "I looked at the data, and I just know." Would you trust their prescription? What if their diagnosis was about you or a loved one? This is the "black box" problem, one of the most significant hurdles to deploying machine learning systems in the real world. A model that produces a prediction without an explanation is often a liability. In high-stakes environments, a correct answer is not enough; you must also be able to show your work. This is where the disciplines of model interpretability and explainability come in. While often used interchangeably, they represent two distinct approaches to understanding a model's behavior.

Defining the Terms: Interpretability vs. Explainability

Understanding the difference between these two concepts is the first step toward building trustworthy AI systems.

Interpretability (The White Box)

Interpretability means that a model's internal mechanics are inherently understandable by a human. You can examine its structure and parameters to understand how it maps inputs to outputs. It is transparent by design.

The Analogy: An interpretable model is like a simple recipe. You can read the list of ingredients, the exact measurements, and the step-by-step instructions. You can follow the logic from start to finish and understand exactly how the final dish was made.

The models:

- **Linear and Logistic Regression:** These are the classic white-box models. The learned coefficients directly tell you about the relationship between each feature and the outcome.

A positive coefficient for 'house size' in a price prediction model means that, all else being equal, a larger house leads to a higher predicted price.

- **Decision Trees:** A single decision tree is a flowchart of if-then-else rules. You can literally trace a single data point's path down the tree to see exactly why it received its final prediction.

Explainability (The Black Box)

Explainability applies to models whose internal workings are too complex for a human to understand directly (e.g., a neural network with millions of weights). Explainability is the use of *post-hoc* (after-the-fact) techniques to approximate and explain a single, individual prediction.

- **The Analogy:** Explainability is like asking a master chef why their incredibly complex, 200-ingredient sauce tastes so good. They can't give you a simple recipe, but they can taste it and give you a local explanation: "For this specific spoonful, the hint of saffron is bringing out the sweetness of the tomatoes, and the dash of smoked paprika adds that finishing note." You get a brilliant explanation for a specific outcome, but you don't understand the entire system.

- **The Models:** These are typically the highest-performing models, such as **Deep Neural Networks** and complex **Gradient Boosting models (e.g., XGBoost)**.

- **The Techniques:** The explanation is not provided by the model itself, but by a separate tool that analyzes the model's behavior. The most common techniques are **LIME** and **SHAP**, which we'll preview shortly.

Why This Matters in Production: The Business Case for 'Why'

In the lab, the pursuit of higher accuracy often justifies the use of a black box. In production, the need for 'why' is often a critical business requirement.

Building Trust: Stakeholders, doctors, loan officers, marketers, and customers are far more likely to trust and adopt a model's recommendation if they can understand its reasoning. An explanation, even a simplified one, is the bridge between a probabilistic output and human trust.

- **Debugging and Model Improvement:** When a model makes a strange or incorrect prediction, explainability tools are your best friends for debugging. We once worked on a model where local explanations for some bad predictions consistently highlighted a seemingly random ID column as the most important feature. This made no sense. After digging in, we discovered a data leakage problem: the ID was inadvertently correlated with the target variable in the training set. The explainability tool didn't just tell us the prediction was wrong; it pointed us directly to the bug in the feature engineering pipeline.

- **Compliance and Legal Requirements:** In many industries, this is a non-negotiable requirement. As discussed in the loan model field story, laws such as the **Equal Credit Opportunity Act (ECOA)** in the US require you to provide a specific reason for denying someone credit. GDPR in Europe includes a "right to an explanation" for automated decisions. A black box model, no matter how accurate, may be illegal to deploy in these contexts.

- **Fairness and Bias Detection:** How do you know if your model is fair? Explainability techniques can help you uncover if a model is relying on sensitive or proxy features. For example, an explainer might reveal that a loan model is heavily penalizing applicants from a certain zip code. While 'zip code' is not a protected class, it can be a strong proxy for race. Uncovering this allows you to debug and mitigate the model's bias.

A Preview of Common Techniques

We will do a deep dive into XAI (Explainable AI) techniques in Chapter 7, but it's important to introduce the two main categories of explanations here.

Global Explanations: How the Model Works Overall

These techniques explain the model's average behavior across the entire dataset. The most common is **Feature Importance**, which assigns a score to each feature based on its overall contribution to the model's predictions. It answers the question: "In general, what features does my model care about the most?"

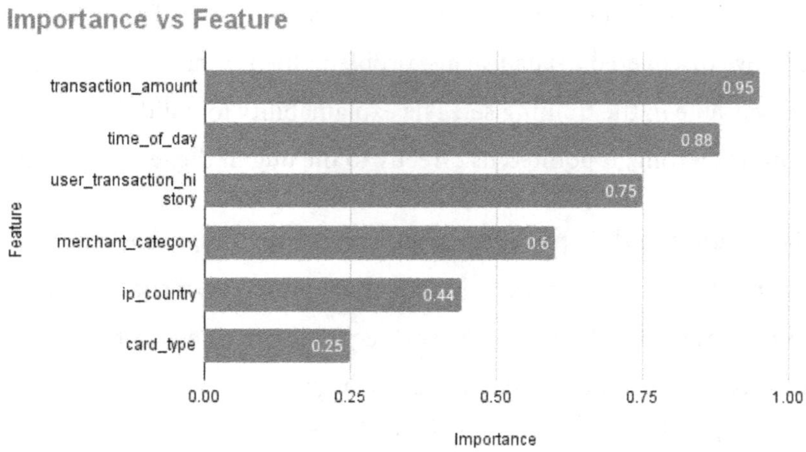

Figure 3.7. A typical feature-importance plot showing the most influential feature.

Local Explanations: Why This One Prediction?

These techniques are the core of modern explainability, focusing on a single prediction.

- **LIME (Local Interpretable Model-agnostic Explanations):** The core idea is clever and intuitive. To explain why a complex model made a specific prediction, LIME creates a tiny, temporary "imitation" model (like a simple linear regression) that is only trained on the data points in the immediate vicinity of that one prediction. Because the imitation model is simple, it's interpretable, and it gives a good local approximation of the black box's behavior.

- **SHAP (SHapley Additive exPlanations):** This is currently the most robust and popular method. It uses a concept from cooperative game theory, the Shapley values, to fairly distribute the "payout" (the prediction) among the "players" (the features). For each prediction, SHAP tells you exactly how much each feature's value contributed to pushing the prediction away from the baseline average.

Interpretability and Explainability are not just academic exercises; they are critical features of a robust, trustworthy, and maintainable data product. The deployed data scientist doesn't just build accurate models; they build understandable ones.

Comprehensive Explainability Framework

Understanding that you need to explain your models is the very first step. The next step is to build a systematic practice for doing so. A single explainability technique is not enough. To build true trust and diagnostic power, you need a comprehensive framework that lets you inspect your model from multiple angles, from the 30,000-foot view of its overall behavior down to the ground-level reasons for a single prediction. Think of it like diagnosing a car. You need the high-level spec sheet that tells you the engine's average horsepower (a global view). Still, you also need a diagnostic computer that can trace a specific engine knock back to a single faulty spark plug (a local view). A complete framework provides both. I structure this framework into three layers.

Layer 1: Global Model Behavior (The 30,000-Foot View)

This layer is about understanding the model's overall logic and the most important patterns it learned from the data. It's your first-pass sanity check after training a model. **The Question it Answers:** "In general, what does my model care about, and what relationships did it learn?"

Technique 1: Feature Importance

This is the most common and fundamental global explanation. It assigns a score to each feature based on its overall contribution to the model's predictions across the entire dataset. It is the first thing you should look at after training any tree-based model or other complex classifier. If your churn model's most important feature is 'customer ID', you know you have a data leakage problem.

Technique 2: Partial Dependence Plots (PDP)

While feature importance tells you *which* features are important, a PDP tells you *how important each* feature is. A PDP shows the marginal effect of one or two features on the predicted outcome, while averaging out the effects of all other features. **It answers the question**: "Holding everything else constant, how does the model's prediction change as I vary *this one feature*?" For a house price model, the PDP for 'square footage' would likely show a positive, upward-sloping line, confirming the sensible relationship that as size increases, so does the predicted price.

Layer 2: Local Prediction Explanations

This layer is about debugging and building trust. It focuses on explaining one specific prediction at a time. **The Question it Answers:** "Why did my model give *this specific customer* this score?"

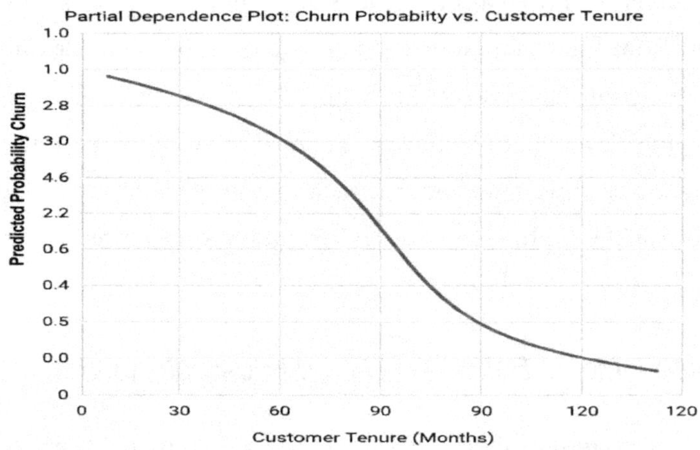

Figure 3.8. A Partial Dependence Plot.

Technique: SHAP (Shapley Additive exPlanations)

While other local explainers like LIME exist, SHAP has become the industry standard for its robustness and theoretical foundations. It uses a concept from game theory to fairly attribute the "payout" (the prediction) among the "players" (the features).

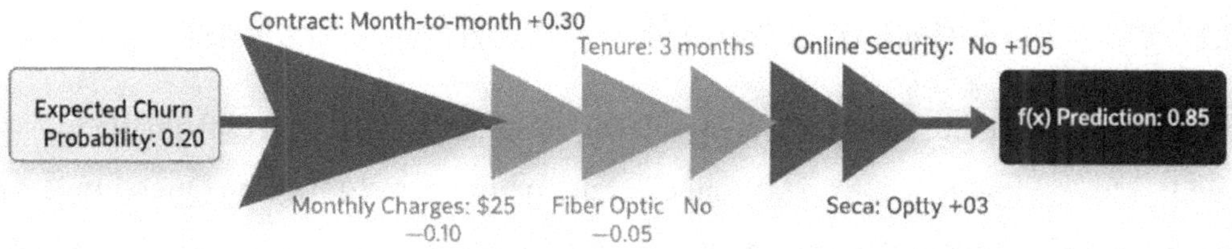

Figure 3.9. A SHAP force plot for Customer Churn.

For each prediction, SHAP assigns each feature a value that represents how much that feature contributed to pushing the prediction away from the baseline average. The best way to visualize this is with a SHAP "force plot." The force plot is incredibly intuitive. It shows a baseline (the average prediction across all data) and displays the features as forces that push the prediction higher (in red) or lower (in blue). It provides a complete, quantitative accounting for a single prediction. Let's analyze a hypothetical customer who is predicted to have a high probability of churning.

- **Base Value**: The average churn probability for all customers is 0.15.
- **Positive Forces (Red)**:
    - The feature Contract = Month-to-month provides the strongest push towards churning.
    - The feature Tenure = 2 months also increases the churn risk, as new customers are more likely to leave.
- **Negative Forces (Blue):**
    - The feature Internet Service = No lowers the prediction, as customers without this service might be less likely to churn.
- **Final Prediction**: After combining the base value with all the positive and negative forces, the model's final prediction for this customer is a **churn probability of 0.82.**

This visualization makes it clear that the customer's month-to-month contract is the primary reason the model predicts they will churn.

Layer 3: Counterfactual Explanations (The "What-If" Analysis)

This is the most advanced but most user-centric layer of explanation. It moves from diagnosis ("Why was I denied?") to actionable recourse ("What can I do to be approved?"). **The Question it Answers:** "What is the smallest change I can make to my inputs to flip the model's prediction?" A counterfactual explanation provides a path to a different outcome. Consider the loan denial example:

Model Prediction: "Loan denied for Ankit Anand."

SHAP Explanation (The 'Why'): "Because your credit utilization is high (pushes score down) and your income is low for the requested loan amount (pushes score down)." This is diagnostic.

Counterfactual Explanation (The 'How'): "To get your loan approved, you would need to either **decrease your credit utilization from 85% to below 50%** or **increase your annual income by $10,000**." This is actionable. Counterfactuals are the key to building truly fair and human-centric AI systems. They empower the end user by providing a clear, achievable path forward, transforming the model from an opaque judge into a helpful guide.

Putting it all Together: The Explainability Workflow

A deployed data scientist uses these three layers together in a continuous workflow:

1. **After Training (Global):** You first check the global feature importance and key PDPs. Does the model's overall logic make sense? Is it relying on sensible features? This is your high-level sanity check.

2. **During Debugging (Local):** When you encounter a surprising or incorrect prediction in your validation set or in production, you generate a local SHAP plot. Which features were responsible for this specific error? This is your deep-dive diagnostic tool.

3. **For End-Users (Counterfactual):** When your model's decision is presented to an end-user (like a customer or an internal business partner), you provide a counterfactual explanation to give them actionable recourse.

By employing a comprehensive framework that combines global, local, and counterfactual explanations, you can turn a black-box model into a trustworthy, transparent, and actionable data product.

```
import shap
import lime
import lime.lime_tabular
import matplotlib.pyplot as plt
from typing import List, Dict
import pandas as pd
import numpy as np
class ModelExplainer:
    """Comprehensive model explanation framework"""
    def __init__(self, model, feature_names: List[str], class_names: List[str] = None):
        self.model = model
        self.feature_names = feature_names
        self.class_names = class_names or ['Class 0', 'Class 1']
        # Initialize explainers
        self.shap_explainer = self._init_shap_explainer()
        self.lime_explainer = self._init_lime_explainer()
    def _init_shap_explainer(self):
        """Initialize appropriate SHAP explainer based on model type"""
        try:
            if hasattr(self.model, 'predict_proba'):
                return shap.TreeExplainer(self.model)
            else:
                return shap.KernelExplainer(self.model.predict, shap.sample(X, 100))
        except:
            return shap.LinearExplainer(self.model, X)
    def _init_lime_explainer(self):
        """Initialize LIME explainer"""
        return lime.lime_tabular.LimeTabularExplainer(
            training_data=X,
            # Should be passed from training data
            feature_names=self.feature_names, class_names=self.class_names, mode='classification')
    def global_explanations(self, X: pd.DataFrame) -> Dict:
        """Generate global model explanations"""
        explanations = {}
        # SHAP summary plot
        shap_values = self.shap_explainer.shap_values(X)
        explanations['shap_summary'] = self._create_shap_summary(shap_values, X)
        # Feature importance
        explanations['feature_importance'] = self._calculate_feature_importance(shap_values)
        # Partial dependence plots
        explanations['partial_dependence'] = self._calculate_partial_dependence(X)
        return explanations
    def local_explanations(self, instance: np.ndarray, num_features: int = 10) -> Dict:
        """Generate local explanations for a single instance"""
        explanations = {}
        # SHAP local explanation
        shap_local = self.shap_explainer.shap_values(instance.reshape(1, -1))
        explanations['shap_local'] = self._format_shap_local(shap_local, instance)
        # LIME explanation
        lime_exp = self.lime_explainer.explain_instance(
            instance, self.model.predict_proba, num_features=num_features)
        explanations['lime_explanation'] = lime_exp.as_list()
        # Anchors (if available)
```

```
        try:
            from alibi.explainers import AnchorTabular
            anchor_explainer = AnchorTabular(
                self.model.predict, feature_names=self.feature_names)
            anchor_explainer.fit(X)
            # Training data
            anchor_exp = anchor_explainer.explain(instance)
            explanations['anchor_explanation'] = anchor_exp.anchor
        except ImportError:
            explanations['anchor_explanation'] = "Anchors not available"
        return explanations
    def generate_explanation_report(self, X: pd.DataFrame, instances: List[int] = None) -> Dict:
        """Generate comprehensive explanation report"""
        if instances is None:
            instances = [0, 1]  # Default to first two instances
        report = {
            'global_explanations': self.global_explanations(X),
            'local_explanations': {},
            'fairness': self._assess_fairness(X),
            'explanation_metrics': self._calculate_explanation_metrics(X)}
        for idx in instances:
            if idx < len(X):
                report['local_explanations'][f'instance_{idx}'] = self.local_explanations(X.iloc[idx].values)
        return report
# Model-specific interpretability
class InterpretabilityFactory:
    """Factory for model-specific interpretability techniques"""
    @staticmethod
    def create_explainer(model, model_type: str, kwargs):
        """Create appropriate explainer based on model type"""
        explainers = {
            'tree': TreeModelExplainer,
            'linear': LinearModelExplainer,
            'neural_network': NeuralNetworkExplainer,
            'ensemble': EnsembleModelExplainer}
        if model_type not in explainers:
            raise ValueError(f"Unsupported model type: {model_type}")
        return explainers[model_type](model, kwargs)
class TreeModelExplainer:
    """Specialized explainer for tree-based models"""
    def __init__(self, model, feature_names: List[str]):
        self.model = model
        self.feature_names = feature_names
    def get_tree_structure(self, tree_index: int = 0) -> Dict:
        """Extract and explain tree structure"""
        if hasattr(self.model, 'estimators_'):
            tree = self.model.estimators_[tree_index].tree_
        else:
            tree = self.model.tree_
        return {
            'nodes': tree.node_count,
            'max_depth': tree.max_depth,
            'feature_importance': self._extract_tree_importance(tree),
            'decision_paths': self._extract_decision_paths(tree)}
    def _extract_tree_importance(self, tree) -> Dict:
        """Extract feature importance from tree structure"""
        importance = {}
        for i, feature in enumerate(self.feature_names):
            importance[feature] = tree.compute_feature_importances(normalize=False)[i]
        return importance
```

Listing 3.7: Model interpretability framework.

Field Story: The Hyperparameter Nightmare

The incident began as a routine model update. The customer's segmentation model had been performing well, but the team identified opportunities for improvement through hyperparameter optimization. Little did we know that this routine update would teach us one of the most valuable lessons in production ML. The team implemented a sophisticated hyperparameter optimization framework:

```
import optuna
from typing import Dict
from sklearn.ensemble import RandomForestClassifier
from sklearn.model_selection import cross_val_score

class HyperparameterOptimizer:
    """Advanced hyperparameter optimization with constraints"""
    def __init__(self, X_train, y_train, model_class, fixed_params: Dict):
        self.X_train = X_train
        self.y_train = y_train
        self.model_class = model_class
        self.fixed_params = fixed_params
        self.study = None

    def optimize(self, n_trials: int = 100, timeout: int = 3600) -> Dict:
        """Run hyperparameter optimization"""
        self.study = optuna.create_study(
            direction='maximize', sampler=optuna.samplers.TPESampler(),
            pruner=optuna.pruners.HyperbandPruner())
        self.study.optimize(self._objective, n_trials=n_trials, timeout=timeout)
        return {
            'best_params': self.study.best_params,
            'best_value': self.study.best_value,
            'trials_data': self.study.trials_dataframe(),
            'optimization history': self._get_optimization_history()}
    def _objective(self, trial) -> float:
        """Objective function for optimization"""
        # Define hyperparameter search space
        params = {
            'n_estimators': trial.suggest_int('n_estimators', 100, 1000),
            'max_depth': trial.suggest_int('max_depth', 3, 20),
            'min_samples_split': trial.suggest_int('min_samples_split', 2, 20),
            'min_samples_leaf': trial.suggest_int('min_samples_leaf', 1, 10),
            'max_features': trial.suggest_categorical('max_features', ['sqrt', 'log2', None])}
        # Combine with fixed parameters
        all_params = {**params, **self.fixed_params}
        # Create and evaluate model
        model = self.model_class(**all_params)
        # Cross-validation with business metrics
        scores = cross_val_score(model, self.X_train, self.y_train,
                                 cv=5, scoring='f1_macro')
        # Add constraints
        training_time = self._measure_training_time(model)
        if training_time > 300:  # 5 minutes constraint
            trial.set_user_attr('training_time_violation', True)
            return float('-inf')
        return scores.mean()
    def _measure_training_time(self, model) -> float:
        """Measure training time for constraint checking"""
        import time
        start_time = time.time()
        model.fit(self.X_train, self.y_train)
        return time.time() - start_time_
```

Listing 3.8: Hyperparameter optimization setup.

The Silent Failure

The optimization identified parameters that improved the validation F1-score by 3%. We deployed the new model with confidence. Within hours, the team received reports of strange segmentations. The issue wasn't in the code or the optimization algorithm. The problem was more subtle:

- **Over-optimization**: We optimized for the F1-score without considering business constraints.
- **Feature sensitivity**: The new parameters made the model overly sensitive to minor variations in features.
- **Distribution shift**: The validation set didn't fully reflect the data distribution.

We implemented a more robust optimization framework:

```
from abc import ABC, abstractmethod
import numpy as np
class HyperparameterOptimizer(ABC):
    """Base class for hyperparameter optimization"""
    def __init__(self, model_class, fixed_params=None):
        self.model_class = model_class
        self.fixed_params = fixed_params or {}
    @abstractmethod
    def _suggest_parameters(self, trial):
        pass
class RobustHyperparameterOptimizer(HyperparameterOptimizer):
    """Hyperparameter optimization with robustness checks"""
    def _objective(self, trial) -> float:
        """Robust objective function with multiple validation sets"""
        params = self._suggest_parameters(trial)
        all_params = {**params, **self.fixed_params}
        model = self.model_class(all_params)
        # Multiple validation strategies
        scores = []
        # Temporal validation
        temporal_score = self._temporal_validation(model)
        scores.append(temporal_score)
        # Geographical validation
        geo_score = self._geographical_validation(model)
        scores.append(geo_score)
        # Adversarial validation
        adv_score = self._adversarial_validation(model)
        scores.append(adv_score)
        # Business metric validation
        business_score = self._business_metric_validation(model)
        scores.append(business_score)
        # Weighted combination with robustness penalty
        base_score = np.mean(scores)
        robustness_penalty = np.std(scores) * 0.5  # Penalize high variance
        return base_score - robustness_penalty
    def _temporal_validation(self, model) -> float:
        """Validate on different time periods"""
        # Implementation for time-based validation
        pass
    def _business_metric_validation(self, model) -> float:
        """Validate using business metrics instead of pure accuracy"""
        # Convert technical metrics to business value
        pass
```

Listing 3.9: Robust hyperparameter optimization.

Key Principles for Production Model Engineering

1. **Reproducibility First**: Every experiment must be fully reproducible.
2. **Business Alignment**: Technical metrics must translate to business value.
3. **Robustness over Optimization**: Prefer stable models over peak performers.
4. **Transparency by Design**: Build explainability into the modeling process.
5. **Continuous Validation**: Validate across multiple dimensions and scenarios.
6. **Governance and Compliance**: Implement proper version control and approval workflows.

In the next chapter, we'll explore automating the journey from model development to production deployment through pipelines.

Chapter Summary

With a data strategy in place, this chapter focused on the craft of building a production-ready model. We learned that the "best" model is rarely the one with the highest accuracy, but the one that is the most balanced, trustworthy, and auditable. This chapter was about building the core artifact, the model itself, with an engineer's discipline. We moved from a simple leaderboard to a holistic view of what makes a model truly "production-ready."

- **Model Selection is a Business Trade-off:** The Model Selection Decision Framework taught us to choose models by balancing performance (accuracy) against interpretability, operational cost (latency, size), and maintainability.
- **Accuracy is a Vanity Metric:** For real-world (imbalanced) data, we must use advanced metrics like **Precision, Recall, F1-Score,** and **ROC-AUC** to get a true picture of a model's performance.
- **The Model Registry is Your Single Source of Truth:** To avoid the chaos of file- based management, a model registry is essential. It provides the "Git for models," delivering version control, lineage, and governance.
- **Explainability (XAI) is a Feature:** We must build models that are not black boxes. Using tools like **SHAP** and **LIME** is critical for debugging, regulatory compliance, and building stakeholder trust.

- The key insight is that model engineering is as much about process and governance as it is about algorithms and mathematics. The most sophisticated model will fail in production without proper engineering discipline.

CHAPTER 4

Your Automated Assembly Line to Production

So far, we have forged a production-ready model. It's built on a solid data strategy, chosen with a rigorous decision framework, and versioned in the model registry. It is a powerful artifact, a masterpiece of potential, but it's currently an engine sitting on a workbench in the garage.

The next critical step is to build the automated assembly line that can safely and reliably take that engine, place it in the chassis of the application, and roll it out to the world. This process, powered by **Continuous Integration** (CI) and **Continuous Delivery** (CD), transforms a workflow from a series of manual, error-prone steps into a highly efficient, automated, and boringly reliable system.

This automation is not just for efficiency; it is for reliability, consistency, and velocity. It's what allows your data product to evolve and adapt at the speed of the business.

The Role of Containerization: Docker and Kubernetes

Before we can build the pipeline, we must solve one of the oldest and most frustrating problems in software development: the dreaded "**but it works on my machine**!" curse. Have you experienced it? Your code runs perfectly on your MacBook, but when your colleague tries to run it on their

Windows machine or when you deploy it to a Linux server in the cloud, it crashes because of a missing dependency, a different Python version, or some other environmental mismatch.

This problem is exacerbated in data science, where complex dependencies on specific library versions, such as TensorFlow, PyTorch, and CUDA, make maintenance difficult. The solution that has become the industry standard is **containerization**, and the undisputed king of containerization is **Docker**.

Docker: The Standardized Shipping Container

The genius of Docker lies in its analogy to a physical shipping container. Before standardized containers, shipping was a chaotic nightmare. Goods of all shapes and sizes had to be loaded and unloaded manually. The shipping container solved this by putting everything, bananas, cars, or electronics, into a standard-sized box with standard connectors. Now, any port in the world with the right crane can move any container, regardless of what's inside. A Docker container does the exact same thing for software. It packages your application code (e.g., your Python prediction service) along with *all* its dependencies; the specific Python version, the required libraries from 'requirements.txt', system libraries, and environment variables; into a single, immutable artifact called an image. This image can then be run as a container on any machine with Docker installed, and it will run the same way every time. You define how to build this image using a simple text file called a 'Dockerfile'.

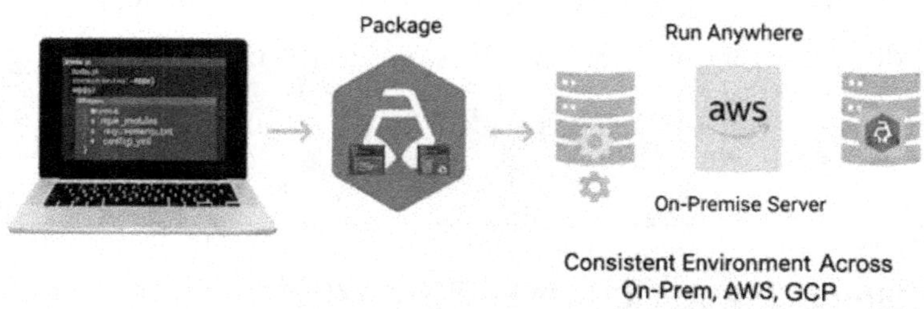

Figure 4.1. Docker solves the "it works on my machine" problem by packaging an application and its dependencies into a single, portable container.

Here is a basic 'Dockerfile' for a Python/FastAPI service that serves a scikit-learn model:

```
# Use an official Python runtime as a parent image
FROM python:3.9-slim
# Set the working directory in the container
WORKDIR /app
# Copy the dependencies file and install them
COPY requirements.txt .
RUN pip install --no-cache-dir -r requirements.txt
# Copy the rest of the application code into the container
COPY..
# Tell Docker what command to run when the container
starts
# This will start the FastAPI server on port 8000
CMD ["uvicorn", "main: app", "--host", "0.0.0.0", "--port", "8000"]
```

Listing 4.1: Dockerfile for a Python/FastAPI service.

This simple file is a complete, reproducible blueprint for your application. It eliminates environmental drift and is the foundational building block of any modern CI/CD pipeline.

Kubernetes: The Global Port Authority

If Docker gives us the standardized shipping container, **Kubernetes** gives us the global port authority and automated crane system. It is an open-source container orchestration platform that manages, scales, and heals its containerized applications. While a single container is easy to run, what happens when you need to run hundreds of containers to handle production traffic?

- How do you distribute traffic between them? (Networking and Load Balancing)
- How do you automatically add more containers when traffic spikes, and remove them when it subsides? (Scaling)
- What happens if a server crashes and its containers die? (Self-Healing)

Kubernetes solves these problems. You declare the desired state of your application (e.g., "I want to run 3 replicas of my fraud detection service and expose it to the internet on port 443"), and Kubernetes works continuously to make that state a reality. It is, in effect, the operating system for the cloud. All major cloud providers offer managed Kubernetes services that handle the complex setup for you: **Amazon EKS**, **Google GKE**, and **Azure AKS**.

As a deployed data scientist, you don't need to be a Kubernetes expert, but you need to understand that your Dockerized application will almost certainly be running on it. This is the environment your CI/CD pipeline will ultimately be deploying to.

The ML Testing Pyramid: A Stratified Defense

As a developer at heart, the one thing that gives us confidence in a complex system is a good test suite. In the chaotic world of machine learning, where data, models, and code are all in flux, a robust testing strategy isn't just a best practice; it's the only thing that will let you sleep at night.

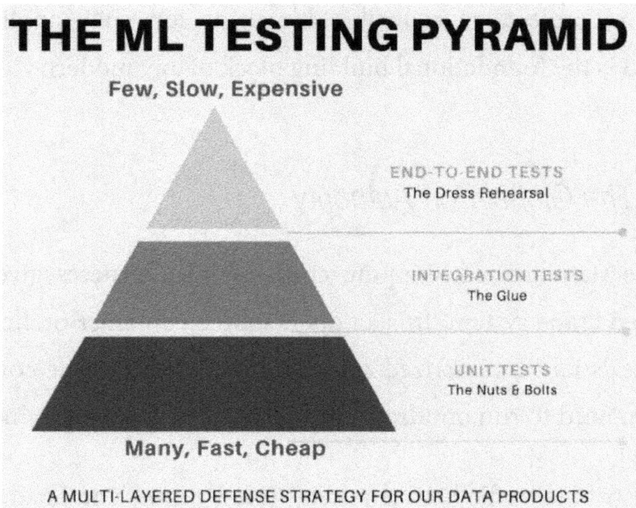

Figure 4.2. The ML Testing Pyramid: a multi-layered defense strategy for their data products.

But not all tests are created equal. Running a full, end-to-end model training pipeline on every single code change is slow, expensive, and wildly inefficient. The software engineering community solved this problem decades ago with the concept of the "testing pyramid." We're going to adapt this proven idea for the unique challenges of our MLOps world. Think of it as a stratified defense system for your data product. The broad base of the pyramid consists of thousands of cheap, fast tests that catch simple, stupid mistakes instantly. As you move up the pyramid, the tests become more complex, slower, and more expensive, but they catch a different class of system-wide failure.

Layer 1: Unit Tests (The Nuts and Bolts)

This is our home turf as developers. Unit tests are the foundation of the pyramid. They are small, lightning-fast, and designed to test a single function or component in complete isolation from the rest of the system. Your goal is simple: to verify that the individual nuts and bolts of your application work exactly as intended.

What to Test: Pure-logic functions in your feature engineering scripts, data cleaning utilities, and validation helpers.

Key Principle: These tests should have *no external dependencies.* They don't read from a real database, they don't call a real API, and they don't touch a real file system. They test pure logic, and that's why they're so fast.

```
from datetime import date
def calculate_age(date_of_birth: date) -> int:
    """Calculates age from date of birth."""
    today = date.today()
    if date_of_birth > today:
        raise ValueError("Date of birth cannot be in the future.")
    return today.year - date_of_birth.year - ((today.month, today.day) < (date_of_birth.month, date_of_birth.day))
def normalize_text(text: str) -> str:
    """Normalizes text for NLP processing."""
    if not isinstance(text, str):
        return ""
    return text.lower().strip()
# Test: test_feature_engineering.py
import pytest
from feature_engineering import calculate_age, normalize_text
def test_calculate_age_correctly():
    """Test age calculation with a known date."""
    dob = date(1990, 5, 15)
    # This logic correctly handles leap years and birthday timing
    expected_age = (date.today() - dob).days // 365
    assert calculate_age(dob) in [expected_age, expected_age - 1]  # Account for leap day differences
def test_calculate_age_with_future_date_should_raise_value_error():
    """Test that future date raises ValueError."""
    future_dob = date.today().replace(year=date.today().year + 1)
    with pytest.raises(ValueError):
        calculate_age(future_dob)
def test_normalize_text_handles_various_inputs():
    """Test text normalization with padding, case, and nulls."""
    assert normalize_text(" Hello WORLD ") == "hello world"
    assert normalize_text("") == ""
    assert normalize_text(None) == ""
```

Listing 4.2: Unit tests for simple feature engineering functions.

A feature engineering script is full of pure logical functions that are perfect candidates for unit testing. In the example below, we test a function that calculates a user's age and another that normalizes text.

Layer 2: Integration Tests (The Glue)

Our unit tests have proven that the individual nuts and bolts are well-made. Now, we need to test the glue that holds them together. Integration tests verify that the different components of your system work correctly together. This is where we test our data pipelines and workflows.

This layer is our specific defense against the "ghost in the join" and "silent failure" disasters. Does our feature engineering pipeline correctly read a sample CSV, process it through all the functions we just unit-tested, and write a valid Parquet file? That's an integration test.

- **What to Test:** The full feature engineering pipeline, a model training workflow, and interactions with a test database.
- **Key Principle:** These tests interact with real, but temporary, infrastructure, like a local test database running in a Docker container or temporary files on disk.

Example: Testing a Complete Feature Pipeline

This test doesn't check the individual functions. It treats the entire pipeline as a single unit and verifies its overall behavior on a small, controlled input.

```
# test_pipeline_integration.py
import pandas as pd
import tempfile
import os
from my_project.pipeline import run_feature_pipeline
def test_complete_pipeline_integration_with_good_data():
    """Test the entire feature pipeline with a clean, sample CSV."""
    with tempfile.TemporaryDirectory() as tmp_dir:
        # Arrange: Create sample input data
        input_data = pd.DataFrame({
            'user_id': [1, 2, 3],
            'date_of_birth': ['1985-01-15', '1990-06-20', '1995-12-10'],
            'email': ['test1@example.com', 'test2@example.com', 'test3@GMAIL.com']
        })
        input_file = os.path.join(tmp_dir, "test_input.csv")
        output_file = os.path.join(tmp_dir, "test_output.parquet")
        input_data.to_csv(input_file, index=False)
        # Act: Run the complete pipeline
        run_feature_pipeline(input_file, output_file)
        # Assert: Validate the final output
        assert os.path.exists(output_file)
        output_df = pd.read_parquet(output_file)
        # Check that expected features were created
        expected_features = ['age', 'email_domain']
        assert all(feat in output_df.columns for feat in expected_features)
        # Validate data integrity and transformations
        assert len(output_df) == 3
        assert output_df['email_domain'].tolist() == ['example.com', 'example.com', 'gmail.com']
def test_pipeline_handles_missing_data_gracefully():
    """Test that the pipeline doesn't crash on incomplete data."""
    with tempfile.TemporaryDirectory() as tmp_dir:
        input_data = pd.DataFrame({
            'user_id': [1, 2],
            'date_of_birth': [None, '1990-06-20'],  # One missing value
            'email': ['test@example.com', 'invalid-email']
        })
        input_file = os.path.join(tmp_dir, "test_input_missing.csv")
        output_file = os.path.join(tmp_dir, "test_output_missing.parquet")
        input_data.to_csv(input_file, index=False)
        # Act: The pipeline should handle missing data without crashing
        run_feature_pipeline(input_file, output_file)
        # Assert: The output exists and has the correct number of rows
        assert os.path.exists(output_file)
        output_df = pd.read_parquet(output_file)
        assert len(output_df) == 2
```

Listing 4.3: An integration test for an entire feature engineering pipeline.

Layer 3: End-to-End Tests (The Dress Rehearsal)

At the very top of the pyramid are the end-to-end (E2E) tests. These are the final dress rehearsals before the show goes live. An E2E test simulates a real user journey through the complete, deployed system. They are the most comprehensive, but also the slowest, most expensive, and most brittle tests to write and maintain.

For our world, this typically means testing the deployed model API endpoint. We are no longer testing the Python code directly; we are testing the live HTTP service running in a real, deployed environment (like staging).

- **What to Test:** The live prediction API, including its response structure, latency, and error handling.
- **Key Principle:** These tests are black boxes. They know nothing about the internal implementation. They only care if the API behaves as expected from an external user's perspective.

Example: Testing the Deployed Model API

This test uses the 'requests' library to make a real HTTP call to a deployed API endpoint and validates its response.

By implementing this stratified testing approach, you build multiple layers of defense. The unit tests catch bugs in your logic instantly. The integration tests catch bugs in your pipelines before they corrupt your data. And the end-to-end tests provide the final confirmation that your deployed system is working as expected. This is how you build the confidence to ship changes quickly and safely.

```
# test_model_api_e2e.py
import requests
import os
import time
# Best practice: Get the API URL from an environment variable
API_BASE_URL = os.environ.get("STAGING_API_URL", "http://localhost:8000")
def test_prediction_endpoint_happy_path():
    """Test the main prediction endpoint with a valid payload."""
    endpoint = f"{API_BASE_URL}/predict"
    test_payload = {
        "age": 35, "monthly_charges": 75.50, "tenure": 24
    }
    response = requests.post(endpoint, json=test_payload, timeout=5)
    # Assert HTTP response is successful
    assert response.status_code == 200
    response_data = response.json()
    # Assert the response has the expected structure and values
    assert "churn_probability" in response_data
    assert 0 <= response_data["churn_probability"] <= 1
    assert "model_version" in response_data
def test_api_latency_within_sla():
    """Test that the API responds within the Service Level Agreement (SLA)."""
    endpoint = f"{API_BASE_URL}/predict"
    test_payload = {"age": 40, "monthly_charges": 99.99, "tenure": 60}
    start_time = time.time()
    response = requests.post(endpoint, json=test_payload, timeout=2)
    latency = time.time() - start_time
    assert response.status_code == 200
    # Assert that latency is under 200 milliseconds
    assert latency < 0.2, f"API latency {latency:.2f}s exceeds 200ms SLA"
def test_invalid_input_returns_client_error():
    """Test that the API gracefully handles invalid or missing inputs."""
    endpoint = f"{API_BASE_URL}/predict"
    invalid_payload = {"age": 30}  # Missing required fields
    response = requests.post(endpoint, json=invalid_payload, timeout=5)
    # The API should return a 4xx client error (e.g., 422 Unprocessable Entity)
    assert 400 <= response.status_code < 500
    assert "detail" in response.json()  # FastAPI provides detailed error messages_
```

Listing 4.4: An end-to-end test for a deployed model API endpoint.

Continuous Integration (CI): Your Automated Quality Gates

The application and its environment are now neatly packaged in a Docker container, a standardized box ready for the assembly line. Now, we will build the first half of that line: Continuous Integration (CI). In traditional software development, CI is a practice in which developers frequently merge their code changes into a central repository, after which automated builds and tests are run. For a machine learning system, the philosophy is the same, but the execution is far more complex. Their CI pipeline is not just a safety net; it's a series of rigorous, automated **quality gates**. Every single code change, no matter how small, must pass through these gates in sequence before it can even be considered a candidate for deployment. A change to an ML system can introduce errors in the code, the data, or the model's behavior. Therefore, their CI pipeline must have gates to validate all three.

Gate 1: Code Quality and Unit Tests

This is their home turf as developers. This first gate is the fastest and cheapest, designed to catch simple mistakes and enforce good coding hygiene. It answers the question: "Is the code itself well-written and logically sound?"

Linting and Formatting: Automatically check the code for stylistic errors (linting) and ensure it conforms to a standard format (e.g., using tools like 'flake8' and 'black' for Python).

Unit Tests: These are small, isolated tests that check the logic of individual functions, completely independent of any real data.

These tests ensure that the fundamental building blocks of your logic are correct before we even think about involving data.

```
# feature_engineering.py
def clean_email_domain(email: str) -> str:
    """Extracts the domain from an email, or returns 'unknown'."""
    if not isinstance(email, str) or "@" not in email:
        return "unknown"
    domain = email.split("@")[-1]
    return domain.lower() if domain else "unknown"
# test_feature_engineering.py
def test_clean_email_domain():
    assert clean_email_domain("test@google.com") == "google.com"
    assert clean_email_domain("user@YAHOO.CA") == "yahoo.ca"
    assert clean_email_domain("invalid-email") == "unknown"
    assert clean_email_domain(None) == "unknown"
    assert clean_email_domain("user@") == "unknown"_
```

Listing 4.5: Unit tests for simple feature engineering functions.

Gate 2: Data Validation and Contract Testing

This is the first critical, ML-specific gate. It is designed to be the automated guard that would have prevented both the "silent failure" and the "ghost in the join" disasters. It answers the question: "Can your code still handle the data you expect to see in the real world?"

This is where the **Data Contract** we discussed in Chapter 2 comes to life. It's not just a document; it's an executable specification. We use tools like **Great Expectations** to enforce it. The tests at this gate go beyond simply checking for column existence; we validate the statistical properties and quality of the data. This gate acts as the immune system for the data pipeline, catching data quality issues and drift early.

Gate 3: Model Validation and Performance Regression

If the code is sound and the data are valid, we move to the next gate: ensuring that the combination still produces a sane and effective model. It answers the question: "Has your code change negatively impacted the model's predictive performance?"

You don't want to run a full, multi-hour training job in every CI run. Instead, you perform a Performance Regression Test. This involves training your model on a small, fixed, and version-controlled "golden dataset" and comparing its performance to a baseline.

1. The pipeline trains the new code on 'golden training set.csv'.
2. It evaluates the resulting model on 'golden validation set.csv'.
3. It compares the key metric (e.g., AUC score) against the score from the current production model.
4. It fails the build if the performance has dropped by more than a predefined threshold (e.g., 2%).

The logic is simple but powerful: 'assert new modelLauc = (production model auc - 0.02)'. This test doesn't prove the new model is great; it proves that it's *not catastrophically worse*.

Gate 4: Fairness and Bias Testing

An accurate but unfair model is a liability. A modern CI pipeline must include an automated gate to test for bias. This gate answers the question: "Does your model perform equitably across different demographic groups?"

We can automate this by running the trained model against a validation set that contains sensitive attributes (which are NEVER used for training, only for evaluation).

```
from sklearn.metrics import accuracy_score, f1_score
def test_fairness_across_groups(model, X_test, y_test, sensitive_attribute):
    """Test model performance across
    sensitive attributes."""
    group_metrics = {}
    for group in X_test[sensitive_attribute].unique():
        mask = X_test[sensitive_attribute] == group
        X_group, y_group = X_test[mask], y_test[mask]
        preds = model.predict(X_group)
        group_metrics[group] = {
            'accuracy': accuracy_score(y_group, preds),
            'f1': f1_score(y_grcup, preds)
        }
    # Assert that the difference in accuracy between groups is within a small tolerance
    accuracies = [m['accuracy'] for m in group_metrics.values()]
    assert max(accuracies) - min(accuracies) < 0.05, \
        "Unfair performance detected across groups"
```

Listing 4.6: An automated fairness test in a CI pipeline.

Gate 5: Infrastructure and Latency Testing

The final gate before we package the artifact is to ensure the model meets its operational requirements. A model isn't just an algorithm; it's a piece of software that must run efficiently. This gate answers the question: "Can your model run in production without violating its Service Level Agreements (SLAs)?"

These tests, often called "model linting," check the properties of the serialized model artifact itself.

```
import time
import os
def test_inference_latency(model, sample_inputs):
    """Test that inference meets the latency SLA (e.g., 100ms)."""
    start_time = time.time()
    for input_data in sample_inputs:
        _ = model.predict(input_data)
    avg_latency = (time.time() - start_time) / len(sample_inputs)
    assert avg_latency < 0.1, f"Latency {avg_latency:.2f}s exceeds 100ms SLA"
def test_model_size(model_path):
    """Test that the model artifact meets size constraints (e.g., 500MB)."""
    model_size_mb = os.path.getsize(model_path) / (1024 * 1024)
    assert model_size_mb < 500, f"Model size {model_size_mb:.1f}MB is too large"_
```

Listing 4.7: Operational tests for model latency and size.

If a code change successfully passes all five of these gates, the CI pipeline has done its job. It produces its final, blessed artifact: a Docker image. A registered model version with a high degree of confidence that it is safe to deploy.

Continuous Delivery (CD): Your Automated Release Engine

The Continuous Integration (CI) pipeline has acted as a series of rigorous quality gates, culminating in a clean, validated, and packaged artifact. We have a Docker container we can trust. Now, we need to get it to our users. This is the job of the second half of the assembly line: Continuous Delivery and Continuous Deployment (CD).

Delivery vs. Deployment: A Critical Distinction

First, let's clarify the often-confused terminology, as the distinction lies in both automation and risk tolerance.

- **Continuous Delivery:** In this setup, the pipeline automates the entire release process, including building, testing, and deploying to a production-like staging environment. However, the final push to live production requires manual, human approval. It is a **one-**

click deployment. A manager or tech lead reviews the changes and clicks a button to promote the release.

- **Continuous Deployment:** The next level of automation. If the pipeline passes all its automated tests, the change is **automatically deployed to production** without any human intervention.

For most machine learning systems, especially in high-stakes environments, Continuous Delivery is the pragmatic, safe starting point. The probabilistic nature of the models means that a human-in-the-loop for the final go-live decision provides a crucial final sanity check.

Deep Dive: Phased Rollout Strategies for ML

You can never be 100% certain of a model's performance until it sees live, messy, unpredictable production traffic. Phased rollouts are a collection of strategies for de-risking a deployment by exposing a new model to a small subset of traffic first, allowing you to observe its real-world behavior before committing to a full launch.

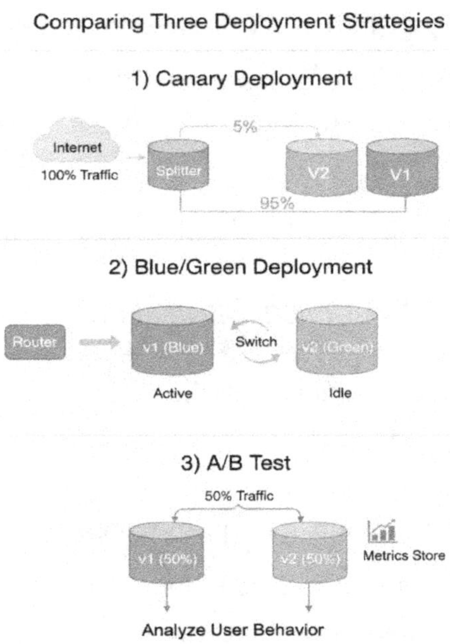

Figure 4.3. Common phased rollout strategies for de-risking model deployments.

Canary Deployment

This is the most common strategy for de-risking technical failures. The new model version (the "canary," as in "canary in a coal mine") is released to a small, controlled subset of users (e.g., 5% of traffic). You then closely monitor its technical metrics.

- **The Goal:** To detect problems like increased latency, higher error rates, or unexpected crashes before they affect many users.
- **The Infrastructure:** Requires an intelligent load balancer, an API Gateway, or a service mesh (such as Istio or Linkerd) that can perform weighted traffic splitting.
- **The Process:** The CD pipeline deploys the canary, waits for a set period (e.g., 15 minutes), and then queries the monitoring system. If the canary's metrics are stable and comparable to the main version, the pipeline automatically increases its traffic to 25%, then 50%, and finally 100%. If the metrics degrade at any point, the pipeline automatically rolls back by setting the canary's traffic weight to 0%.

Blue/Green Deployment

This strategy prioritizes instant rollback and zero downtime, making it ideal for mission-critical applications. It requires you to maintain two identical, parallel production environments, "Blue" and "Green."

- **The Goal:** To provide a zero-downtime deployment with a near-instantaneous, guaranteed rollback path.
- **The Infrastructure:** Requires duplicating your entire production environment (servers, databases, etc.), which can be very expensive. The switch is handled by changing DNS records or reconfiguring a load balancer.
- **The Process:** The current, live model (v1) runs in Blue. The CD pipeline deploys the new model (v2) to the idle Green environment. You can run final, live integration tests against Green without impacting users. When ready, you flip the switch, and all live traffic is

redirected to Green. Blue is kept on standby. If a problem is discovered with v2, you can roll back in seconds by just flipping the switch back to Blue.

A/B Testing (or Champion/Challenger)

This is the gold standard for measuring the *business impact* of a new model. It is less of a deployment safety mechanism and more of an online experimentation framework.

- **The Goal:** To scientifically prove that a new model (the "Challenger") is better than the current one (the "Champion") on a key business metric.

- **The Infrastructure:** Requires a robust experimentation platform capable of segmenting users into groups and a metrics pipeline that can attribute business outcomes (like clicks, purchases, or fraud captures) to the correct model version.

- **The Process:** Users are randomly split, often 50/50, between the two models. The system runs for a statistically significant period (days or weeks) until you can say with confidence that, for example, "Model B increased user engagement by 2%." This data-driven result is what you take to the business to prove the value of your work.

Shadow Deployment (Dark Launching)

This is arguably the safest strategy for testing a new model on real traffic. The new model is deployed "in shadow mode" alongside the old one.

- **The Goal:** To test a new model's performance on 100% of live production traffic without user-facing risk.

- **The Infrastructure:** Requires your service layer to be able to fork production traffic. The live request is sent to *both* models in parallel.

- **The Process:** Only the old (current) model's prediction is returned to the user. The new model's prediction is silently logged. You can then analyze these logs offline to compare the new model's predictions, latency, and error rates with the current model at scale. It is a powerful way to gain confidence in a new model before exposing it to users via a Canary or A/B test.

Deep Dive: The Logic of Automated Rollbacks

An automated rollback is the safety net that makes CD possible. It is a simple but powerful piece of logic in your deployment pipeline that connects it to your monitoring system.

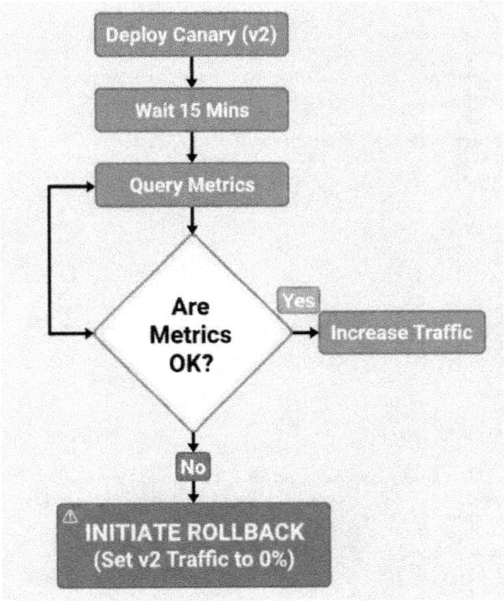

Figure 4.4. The decision logic for an automated canary deployment and rollback.

This closed-loop system: deploy, monitor, and decide, is what gives teams the confidence to release changes quickly and safely.

Building a Modern MLOps Pipeline: Principles and Tools

Pipeline as Code is the core principle. Your entire CI/CD process should be defined in a version-controlled YAML file. This makes it reproducible and auditable. **Modularity** is the other key principle, breaking the pipeline into reusable, self-contained jobs. Here is a more complete, conceptual example of a 'workflow.yml' for GitHub Actions that shows a full CI/CD process with a manual approval gate for production.

```
name: CI/CD Pipeline for Churn Model_
on:
  push:
    branches: ["main"]
jobs:
  test-and-validate:
    runs-on: ubuntu-latest
    steps:
      - name: Code Tests and Validation
        run: |
          # Steps for code tests, data validation, model validation
      - name: Build and Push Docker Image
        run: |
          docker build -t my-registry/churn-model:${{ github.sha }} .
          docker push my-registry/churn-model:${{ github.sha }}
  deploy-to-staging:
    runs-on: ubuntu-latest
    needs: test-and-validate
    environment: staging
    steps:
      - name: Deploy to Staging Environment
        run: |
          kubectl set image deployment/churn-model churn-model=my-registry/churn-model:${{ github.sha }}
      - name: Run Integration Tests
        run: |
          # Run automated tests against the staging endpoint
  approve-for-production:
    runs-on: ubuntu-latest
    needs: deploy-to-staging
    environment:
      name: production
      url: https://my-app.com
    steps:
      - name: Manual approval step
        run: echo "Waiting for manual approval to deploy to production."
  deploy-to-production:
    runs-on: ubuntu-latest
    needs: approve-for-production
    steps:
      - name: Deploy to Production (Canary)
        run: |
          # Command to start a 10% canary release in the production cluster
          kubectl set image deployment/churn-model churn-model=my-registry/churn-model:${{ github.sha }}
          # Logic to manage the canary rollout
```

Listing 4.8: GitHub Actions workflow for ML model CI/CD.

In this workflow, the ‘approve-for-production‘ job will pause the pipeline and wait for a user with the correct permissions to click “Approve” in the GitHub UI before the ‘deploy-to-production’ job is allowed to run. This is a perfect example of Continuous Delivery in practice.

Stories from the Assembly Line

The principles and diagrams we’ve discussed are the blueprints for an automated assembly line. But the true value of this discipline isn’t found in the blueprints; it’s proven in the trenches when the pressure is on. These stories from our careers illustrate the real, tangible impact that a mature CI/CD practice can have on a team, a product, and a business.

Field Story: From 4 Hours of Fear to 30 Minutes of Confidence

One of the most impactful CI/CD pipelines built was for a multi-enterprise consortium in the Master Data Management (MDM) platform, which was a critical, central system of record. For a long time, deploying changes to it was a terrifying, high-stakes ceremony.

The Pain: Deployment as a Ritual of Fear

Before we had a deployed pipeline, a scheduled deployment was a four-hour, after-hours ordeal that required a team of about five people to be on a conference call, usually late on a Friday night. The process was governed by a 50-step manual checklist on a shared spreadsheet. It involved:

1. Manually putting up a maintenance page for the application.
2. Manually running database backup scripts.
3. Stopping services in a precise, required sequence.
4. Manually 'scp'-ing the new application files to the servers.
5. Manually running database migration scripts.
6. Restarting services in another precise sequence.
7. An hour of frantic, manual clicking through the application, trying to verify that they hadn't broken anything.

Everyone hated it. The process was fraught with the risk of human error; a missed step or a typo could bring down a critical system. This created a pervasive "deployment anxiety" throughout the team. We gradually became terrified to release changes. As a result, valuable new features and critical bug fixes were bundled into large, risky, quarterly releases. Innovation was grinding to a halt, not because we couldn't build things, but because we were afraid to ship them.

The Solution: Automating Ourselves Out of a Job

We decided to invest time in building a full CI/CD pipeline using GitHub Actions for orchestration and a Blue/Green strategy on AWS.

- **The CI Half:** We started by building the quality gates. Every 'git push' now automatically triggers a workflow that runs our entire suite of unit and integration tests. We added a data validation gate that checked the core data models against a predefined contract. Only a change that passed every single one of these automated checks could be merged into the main branch. This alone built an incredible amount of confidence.

- **The CD Half:** Once a change was merged, the CD part of the pipeline took over. A team lead could trigger the deployment with a single click. The pipeline would automatically:

    1. Build the new containerized application.
    2. Provision a complete, parallel "Green" environment in AWS.
    3. Deploy the new version of the application to this green environment.
    4. Run a suite of automated smoke tests against the green environment to ensure it is healthy.
    5. If and only if all tests pass, it will automatically switch the production load balancer to point to the green environment. The new version was now live, with zero downtime.

The Impact: More Than Just Speed

The immediate, quantitative impact was a dramatic reduction in deployment time. The four-hour manual ordeal became a 30-minute, fully automated, and frankly, boring process. But the real impact was cultural. The fear of deployment vanished. We went from risky quarterly releases to safe, small, weekly or even daily releases. If a critical hotfix was needed for a bug, we could test it and have it safely in production within an hour during normal business hours.

The CI/CD pipeline didn't just make our process faster; it made the team better. It gave us the confidence to experiment and the freedom to innovate. It freed us from the soul-crushing toil of manual deployments and allowed us to focus on what we were hired to do: build valuable products. That is the true power of this discipline.

Field Story: The Bug That Never Shipped (A CI Story)

Not all victories are as dramatic as a 4-hour deployment shrinking to 30 minutes. Some of the most valuable contributions of a CI pipeline are the disasters that *don't* happen.

- **The Setup:** Fresh off the success with the deployment pipeline, the team was building a new ML model that relied on customer country data. As part of the new CI practice, we had implemented a data validation gate using Great Expectations. One of the checks was a simple but crucial one: the 'country code' column in the customer data must contain one of the accepted values from a predefined list of two-letter ISO codes (['US', 'CA', 'MX', ...]). Some on the team felt it was a bit of overkill. "The data comes from their own CRM," they argued, "it's always going to be in the right format."

- **The Incident:** Two weeks later, a different team that owned the upstream CRM API pushed what they considered a "minor, non-breaking" change. To make the application more user-friendly, we changed the output of the country code field. Instead of the two-letter ISO code (e.g., "US"), API now returns the full country name (e.g., "United States"). We didn't announce this change widely because the API's schema hadn't technically "broken"; the 'country code' field was still there, it was still a string, and it wasn't null.

- **The Catch:** The next morning, a data scientist on my team pushed a completely unrelated change to the model's code. The CI pipeline on GitHub Actions automatically kicked off. Less than five minutes later, it failed. The build was blocked with a bright red 'X'. The error message was crystal clear: the Great Expectations data validation had failed. The values in the 'country code' column no longer matched the 'accepted values' list.

- **The Lesson:** The CI pipeline had caught a silent, data-related bug that would have completely broken the production model. The feature engineering code, which expected a two-letter code to join to a lookup table, would have failed, causing all predictions to fail. Without the automated data validation gate, we would have approved the code change, deployed it, and spent the next day in a frantic fire drill trying to figure out why the model was suddenly crashing.

This small victory was a huge cultural win. It proved that the discipline of data validation and "pipeline thinking" wasn't just academic. It was a real, practical defense mechanism that saved us from a production outage. It was the bug that never shipped!

Chapter Summary

This chapter provided the blueprint for the automated assembly line, the engineering heart of MLOps. We've moved from a manual, artisanal craft to a disciplined, reliable, and automated process for shipping data products.

Here are the key takeaways from building the CI/CD pipeline:

- **Containerization is the Foundation:** Tools like **Docker** are essential. They solve the "it works on my machine" problem by packaging the model, code, and all dependencies into a single, portable artifact, which is the basic unit of deployment.
- **CI is a Multi-Layered Quality Gate:** Continuous Integration for ML is more than just code tests. It's a series of automated gates that validate **code** (unit tests), **data** (data contracts), **models** (performance regression), and **fairness** (bias checks).
- **CD is a Risk-Management Strategy:** Continuous Delivery enables safe, confident releases using phased rollouts. Strategies like **Canary**, **A/B Testing**, and **Shadow Deployments** allow you to test new models on real traffic and measure their impact before a full release.
- **Automation is a Cultural Catalyst:** The ultimate goal of CI/CD is not just speed; it's building team confidence. By automating deployment and rollback procedures, you eliminate manual, error-prone processes, reducing the"fear of deployment" and enabling teams to innovate and ship value faster.

CHAPTER 5

Cloud Infrastructure: Architecting a Home for Your Model

We have now forged a production-ready model from the crucible of data. We've built a robust, automated CI/CD pipeline to test and package it with confidence. We have a perfect, containerized artifact, ready for its journey to the world. But where, exactly, is it going to live?

The answer, for nearly every modern data product, lies in the cloud. Think of it this way: so far, we've designed a revolutionary new car engine (model) and engineered a state-of-the-art robotic assembly line (CI/CD pipeline) to build it. But all of this is currently set up in their personal garage. To truly scale, we need to move out of the garage and into a massive, globally connected industrial park. The cloud is that industrial park. It provides the space, power, security, and global distribution network they need to operate at a scale once impossible. This chapter is not a catalog of cloud services. It is a guide to strategic architecture. We will cover the critical decisions you must make to design a cloud infrastructure that is scalable, secure, cost-effective, and perfectly suited to your data product's needs.

Architecting a Cloud Strategy: Choosing Your Foundation

The cloud is not a single entity; it's a collection of global services offered by major providers like **Amazon Web Services (AWS), Microsoft Azure, Google Cloud Platform (GCP), and Alibaba.**

Your choice of provider will shape your deployment strategy, your available tools, and your team's workflow. The decision is rarely about which provider is "best" in an absolute sense, but rather which one is the best fit for your business needs. A strategic cloud decision is guided by three key factors.

Existing Infrastructure and Team Expertise

This is the most pragmatic, and often most important, factor. The best cloud provider to choose is often the one your company already uses. If your engineering organization has a decade of experience with AWS, and all your existing data already lives in S3, building your MLOps pipeline on AWS SageMaker or EKS will be a faster, cheaper, and more reliable path to production than starting from scratch on GCP. Leveraging existing skills and infrastructure avoids a steep and costly learning curve. Your data scientists can partner with an existing team of cloud experts rather than becoming experts themselves. Never underestimate the power of organizational momentum.

Ecosystem and Specialized Services

Each provider has a different center of gravity and excels in different areas.

- **AWS:** As the oldest and most mature provider, it offers the most extensive and comprehensive ecosystem of services. It has a tool for virtually any need imaginable. Its flagship ML platform, **Amazon SageMaker**, is an incredibly deep and powerful suite of tools that covers the entire MLOps lifecycle, from data labeling to model monitoring.

- **GCP:** Google Cloud's DNA is in data and analytics. With services like **BigQuery** (a best-in- class data warehouse), a world-class Kubernetes engine (GKE), and a strong, AI-first platform in **Vertex AI**, GCP is a natural fit for data-heavy, container-native applications.

- **Azure:** Microsoft's strength lies in the enterprise. Azure integrates seamlessly with existing Microsoft products that many large corporations rely on, like Office 365 and Active Directory. Its **Azure Machine Learning** platform is a mature, robust offering with a strong emphasis on responsible AI and governance, both of which are critical in the corporate world.

Cost and Scalability Models

Cloud costs are not just about the sticker price of a virtual machine; they're about optimizing your architecture for specific workloads. You must understand the difference between:

- **On-Demand Instances:** Like a taxi. You pay a premium for the flexibility to use a server for any amount of time and then shut it down.
- **Reserved Instances:** Like a long-term car lease. You commit to using a server for one or three years and, in return, get a massive discount (up to 70%). This is ideal for stable, predictable workloads.
- **Spot Instances:** Like bidding on an empty seat on an airplane. You can access spare cloud capacity at enormous discounts (up to 90%), but with the catch that the cloud provider can take it back with only a few minutes' notice. This is perfect for fault-tolerant, non-urgent tasks like model training, but terrible for a production inference service.

A good cloud strategy often involves a mix of all three, using the right pricing model for the right job.

The Two Deployment Philosophies: Managed vs. Self-Managed

Once you've chosen a provider, you are faced with your first major architectural decision. How much of the underlying infrastructure do you want to manage yourself? This is the difference between renting a fully equipped factory and building your own from the ground up.

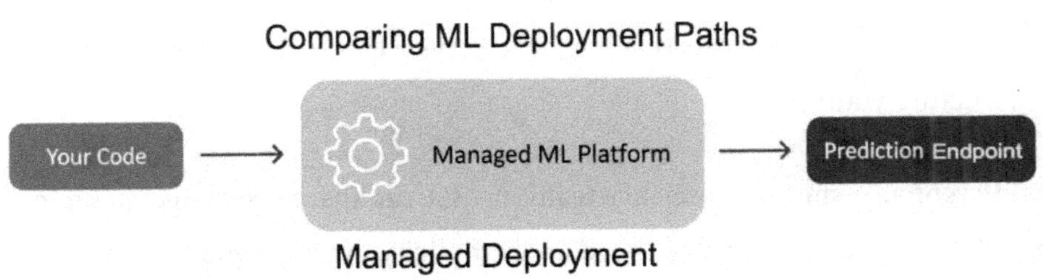

Figure 5.1. Managed Deployment.

The Managed Path: Speed and Simplicity

This is the "renting the factory" approach. Managed ML platforms are services that abstract away almost all the underlying infrastructure. You bring your model code or a trained model artifact, and the service handles the rest: provisioning the servers, configuring the network, setting up a scalable endpoint, and load balancing traffic. Examples: AWS SageMaker Endpoints, Google Cloud Vertex AI Endpoints, and Azure Machine Learning Endpoints.

Pros:

- **Radical Simplicity:** You can often go from a trained model to a production-ready, scalable API endpoint with just a few lines of code or a few clicks in a UI.
- **Faster Time-to-Market:** By abstracting away DevOps complexity, your team can focus on data science rather than infrastructure.
- **Reduced Overhead:** You don't need a dedicated team of Kubernetes experts to manage your model deployments.

Cons:

- **Less Flexibility:** You are constrained by the options the platform provides. If you need a highly custom networking setup or a specific type of hardware, you may be out of luck.
- **Vendor Lock-in:** These platforms are proprietary. The code you write to deploy on SageMaker will not work on Vertex AI. This can make it harder to move to a different cloud provider in the future.
- **Potential Cost at Scale:** While convenient, that convenience comes at a price. At a very large scale, the overhead costs of a managed service can exceed the costs of managing the infrastructure yourself.
- **Ideal Persona:** A small data science team in a startup that needs to get a model into production quickly. They value speed and simplicity over fine-grained control.

The Self-Managed Path: Control and Customization

This is the "building your own factory" approach. Here, you deploy your containerized model to general-purpose compute services. You are responsible for everything: configuring the servers, managing the network, setting up auto-scaling, and monitoring the entire stack.

The industry standard for self-managing containerized applications is **Kubernetes**. All three cloud providers offer excellent managed Kubernetes services that handle the underlying control plane for you: **Amazon EKS (Elastic Kubernetes Service)**, **Google GKE (Google Kubernetes Engine)**, and **Azure AKS (Azure Kubernetes Service)**.

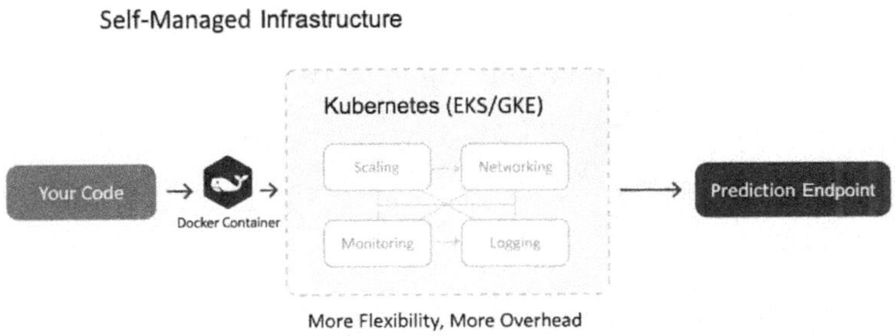

Figure 5.2. Self-Managed Deployment.

Examples: Deploying your Docker container to an EKS cluster, or, for simpler use cases, directly to virtual machines like Amazon EC2.

Pros:

- **Complete Control:** You have granular control over every aspect of the infrastructure, from the machine type to the networking policies. You can fine-tune everything for your specific performance and cost needs.
- **Cost-Effective at Scale:** At a very large scale, managing the infrastructure yourself can be significantly cheaper than paying the premium for a fully managed service.
- **Portable:** Kubernetes is an open-source standard. A deployment configured to run on GKE can be migrated to EKS or AKS with relatively minor changes, avoiding vendor lock-in.

Cons:

- **High Operational Overhead:** This is the biggest drawback. You are now responsible for the security, scaling, and maintenance of your infrastructure. This requires deep DevOps and MLOps expertise. Your data science team will need to be supported by a dedicated platform engineering team.

- **Ideal Persona:** A large tech company with a dedicated MLOps/Platform team that needs to deploy dozens of complex, highly customized models and wants to optimize for performance and cost at a massive scale.

The choice between these two philosophies is one of the most important you will make. It's a fundamental trade-off between speed and control, simplicity and flexibility. There is no single right answer, only the answer that is right for your team's skills, your product's needs, and your company's scale.

Architecting for Performance and Cost: Serverless vs. Dedicated

Once you've chosen your high-level deployment philosophy, managed or self-managed, you face another critical decision at a lower level. How exactly do you want to provision and pay for the computing power that runs your model? This choice is a direct trade-off between performance, cost, and operational simplicity.

The Serverless Approach: The Pay-per-Use Food Truck

Serverless computing is a model where the cloud provider dynamically manages the allocation of machine resources. Your code is packaged into a function that runs only in response to a trigger, such as an API call. You don't manage any servers, and you only pay for the exact compute time you use, down to the millisecond.

The Analogy: A serverless function is like a food truck. The owner parks it, and the engine is off, consuming no fuel. When the first customer of the day arrives (the first request), the owner must start the engine, fire up the grill, and get everything ready. This first meal takes a few extra seconds to prepare. This is the **cold start**. Once the truck is "warm," subsequent orders are served very quickly. If there are no customers for a while, the owner shuts the engine off again to save fuel.

Pros:

- **Extremely Cost-Effective:** If your model is only called a few thousand times a day, this is by far the cheapest option. You pay for a few seconds of compute time rather than for a server running 24/7.
- **Infinite Scaling (in theory):** The cloud provider handles all scaling for you. If you suddenly get a million requests, the platform will automatically spin up a million parallel instances of your function to handle them.

Cons:

- **The Cold Start Problem:** That initial startup delay can range from a few hundred milliseconds to several seconds. This makes serverless unsuitable for applications that require consistent, ultra-low latency, like a real-time fraud detection system.
- **Resource Limits:** Serverless functions have strict limits on execution time (e.g., 15 minutes), memory, and the size of your application package. A massive, multi-gigabyte deep learning model may not fit within these constraints.
- **Examples:** AWS Lambda, Google Cloud Functions, and Azure Functions.

The Dedicated Approach: The Always-On Restaurant

The traditional alternative is to provision a dedicated resource, either a virtual machine or a container, running 24/7 in a cluster, always ready to serve requests.

The Analogy: This is like a traditional restaurant kitchen. It is always on, staffed, and the ovens are hot, even if there are no customers now. When an order comes in, it can be prepared immediately.

Pros:

- **Predictable, Low Latency:** Since the server is always running, there are no cold starts. Every request is served with consistently low latency. This is essential for high-throughput, real-time services.
- **Full Control:** You have full control over the hardware, the operating system, and the runtime environment. There are no arbitrary limits on execution time or memory.

Cons:

- **Higher Cost:** You pay for the server's uptime whether it's receiving requests or sitting idle. This can be very inefficient for sporadic workloads.
- **Management Overhead:** You are responsible for scaling these resources, either manually or by configuring auto-scaling rules based on metrics such as CPU utilization.
- **Examples:** Amazon EC2, Google Compute Engine, Azure Virtual Machines, or containers running in a Kubernetes cluster (EKS, GKE, AKS).

As we'll see in the field story, the best architecture often isn't a choice between one or the other, but a hybrid approach that uses the best tool for each specific job.

The Security Perimeter

Protecting Your Assets in the Cloud

In a world of increasing data breaches, security is paramount. In the cloud, security is not a feature you bolt on at the end; it is a foundational layer that you must architect from the very beginning.

Pillar 1: Network Isolation

Your models and data should never be exposed directly to the public internet unless necessary.

- **Virtual Private Clouds (VPCs):** A VPC is like building a private, gated-off, and isolated section for your factory within the massive industrial park of the cloud. It is your own private network space.

- **Public vs. Private Subnets:** Within your VPC, you should place resources like your databases and model servers in **private subnets**, which have no direct route to or from the internet. The only way to access them is through a controlled gateway, like a load balancer or an API gateway, which you place in a **public subnet**. This drastically reduces your attack surface.

Pillar 2: Access Management (IAM)

As we discussed in Chapter 2, the **Principle of Least Privilege** is your guiding star. Every user and every service should have the absolute minimum set of permissions required to do their job. Use IAM Roles for services and avoid using long-lived secret keys wherever possible.

Pillar 3: Encryption

All data, without exception, must be encrypted.

- **Encryption at Rest:** Data stored in S3, on virtual machine disks, or in databases must be encrypted. All major cloud providers make this as easy as checking a box.

- **Encryption in Transit:** All data moving over the network must be encrypted using TLS/SSL. This prevents eavesdropping.

Pillar 4: Model Intellectual Property

Remember that your trained model weights are your company's valuable intellectual property. They should be stored in a secure, access-controlled location (e.g., a private S3 bucket), encrypted at rest, and accessible only by authorized services via IAM roles. Never store them in a public repository or check them into Git.

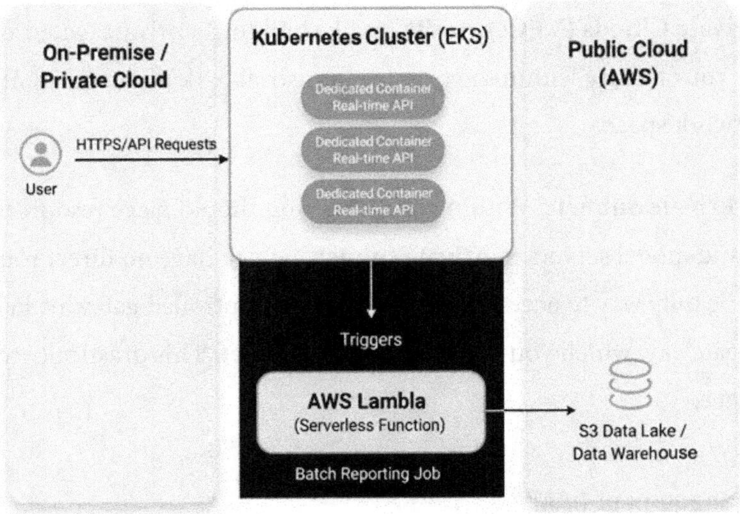

Figure 5.3. A hybrid architecture: using dedicated containers for latency-sensitive services and serverless functions.

Field Story: The Billion-Request Challenge

Our most challenging architectural project involved designing the cloud infrastructure for a massive, multi-tenant Master Data Management (MDM) platform on AWS. The system served as the central source of truth for customer and product data across multiple, distinct business units (their tenants) within a large enterprise.

- **The Challenge:** The system had stringent requirements. It needed to:
    - Handle billions of API requests per month with high availability.
    - Ensure strict, provable data isolation between tenants. Each business unit should have absolutely no way to access another's data.
    - Provide consistently low latency for its core, real-time data retrieval APIs.
- **The Architectural Decisions:** We followed the same decision process we outlined in this chapter.

- **Managed vs. Self-Managed:** A fully managed service, like a traditional SaaS platform, was ruled out early. The cost at that scale would have been astronomical, and more importantly, we could not provide the highly custom, fine-grained control needed for multi-tenant security and performance requirements. We chose the **self-managed path**, building the platform on **Amazon EKS (Kubernetes)**. This gave us the complete control needed.

- **Serverless vs. Dedicated (A Hybrid Approach):** We didn't choose one or the other; we used both. The core, latency-sensitive APIs for reading and writing master data ran on **dedicated** containers within their EKS cluster. These were always on, auto-scaling based on traffic, and optimized for low-latency responses. However, we also had many asynchronous, sporadic background tasks: generating a large export file for a tenant once a day, running a complex data quality report once a week, etc. Running a dedicated 24/7 server for these tasks would have been incredibly wasteful. So, we deployed them as **serverless AWS Lambda functions**. They would spin up, do their job for a few minutes, and spin down, and only paid for those few minutes of compute.

- **The Security Perimeter:** Our highest priority. We used a multi-layered security approach. The entire platform lived in its own VPC. We used separate Kubernetes namespaces and strict network policies to create a logical wall between tenant services. And every microservice had its own, tightly scoped IAM role that granted it only the minimum permissions needed to function.

- **The Lesson** The "right" architecture is rarely a single, pure choice. It is almost always a hybrid. The experience of building that platform taught us that the role of a data architect is to understand the full spectrum of available tools and to make a series of deliberate, defensible trade-offs between cost, performance, control, and security. You use the powerful, always-on dedicated resources where you need speed, and the cost-effective, pay-per-use serverless resources everywhere else.

Chapter Summary

This chapter has served as the guide in building the factory floor for their data products. We've moved from the abstract world of code and models to the concrete, high-stakes decisions of cloud architecture. We've learned that choosing the infrastructure is a strategic exercise in balancing trade-offs.

This chapter was our architectural guide, moving from the "what" to the "where." We've designed the industrial park for data products, focusing on the critical, real-world trade- offs between speed, cost, and control.

- Choosing a cloud provider (AWS, Azure, or GCP) is a strategic decision based on the team's existing expertise, the services ecosystem, and cost models.
- The "Managed Path" (e.g., SageMaker, Vertex AI) offers speed and simplicity but creates vendor lock-in and reduces granular control.
- The "Self-Managed Path" (e.g., Kubernetes on EKS or GKE) provides complete control and better cost-efficiency at scale, but requires significant DevOps expertise.
- Serverless (e.g., AWS Lambda) is highly cost-effective for sporadic workloads but unsuitable for low-latency services due to the "cold start" problem.
- Dedicated instances (e.g., EC2) are the workhorses for high-throughput, real-time APIs that demand consistently low latency.
- A robust security perimeter is non-negotiable and must be designed from the start, using network isolation (VPCs), strict access control (IAM), and encryption for all data.
- The best architectures are often a hybrid, using dedicated resources for low-latency tasks and serverless functions for async.

CHAPTER 6

Model Monitoring and Observability: The Unwavering Watchtower

The Watchtower and the Map of Failures

We may never forget the sinking feeling in our stomach when the VP of Operations called at 2 AM. "Your fancy predictive maintenance model just cost us a $50,000 emergency repair and an angry hospital administrator. The dashboard says everything is fine. What the hell is going on?"

That moment, standing in the kitchen with cold coffee in one hand and a buzzing phone in the other, was a wake-up call. We had deployed what we thought was our most sophisticated model yet: a system to predict HVAC failures in commercial buildings. For six weeks, dashboards showed nothing but green. Accuracy: 98%. Latency: under 100ms. Uptime: 99.99%. By every metric tracked, we were crushing it.

But we learned the hard way that metrics can be beautiful liars.

The reality was that our model had been silently failing for weeks. It was still making predictions, still returning results quickly, still technically "working." But the world around it had changed in ways we never anticipated. New building management software had rolled out, changing how sensor data was reported. Seasonal temperature shifts had altered normal operating patterns. Our model, trained on a static snapshot of history, was now navigating a river that had changed its course.

Deployment isn't the finish line; it's where the real race begins. For months, you've lived in the comfortable, predictable world of development. You've wrestled with messy data, engineered clever features, tuned hyperparameters, and finally achieved that magical accuracy number that makes you feel like you've conquered machine learning. You've navigated the organizational maze, secured approvals, and finally pushed your creation into production. The temptation to dust off your hands, mark the Jira ticket as "done", and dive into the next exciting project is overwhelming.

Resist that temptation. It's the most dangerous mistake you can make in your data science career. Think of your deployed model like the Mars Rover. It was built and tested in the pristine, controlled environment of NASA's clean room. Every component was checked, every scenario simulated. But the moment it landed on Mars, it entered an environment full of unknowns: unexpected dust storms, strange rock formations, temperature variations beyond what they predicted. Without constant communication with mission control and the ability to diagnose new problems, it would quickly become a very expensive paperweight.

Your model is no different. The moment it goes live, it faces solar winds of shifting user behavior, asteroid fields of upstream data changes, and the subtle gravitational pull of its own decaying assumptions. Your most critical post-deployment responsibility is to build that mission control center, an unwavering watchtower that doesn't just watch for problems but helps you understand them.

From Monitoring to Observability: A Critical Distinction

Early in our careers, we thought we understood monitoring. We'd proudly show clients "wall of green", dozens of dashboards tracking every metric we could think of. Then we had an incident that taught the difference between watching and understanding.

We were running a recommendation engine for a major retail client. One morning, the conversion rate dropped by 20%. Our monitoring system dutifully alerted us. But here's what it couldn't tell: *why*.

For eight frantic hours, we chased ghosts. Was it a model? Infrastructure? Data pipelines? Everything looked perfect. The real cause turned out to be completely outside the view: the client's marketing team had launched a new email campaign targeting an older demographic that interacted with products differently than the training data reflected.

That experience taught us that monitoring and observability, while often used interchangeably, represent completely different mindsets.

Monitoring: The Check Engine Light

Monitoring is what most teams start with. It's about answering known questions with predefined metrics. You anticipate how your system might fail and create dashboards to monitor each potential failure.

- How long does a prediction take? *You track latency.*
- How many requests are they serving? *You track throughput.*
- What's their model's accuracy? *You track performance metrics.*

Monitoring is essential, like the check engine light in your car. When it turns on, you know *something* is wrong. But you don't know if it's a loose gas cap or a failing transmission. The light can't tell you; it can only tell you to worry.

At an HVAC Manufacturing Company, we had a beautiful monitoring dashboard for the HVAC optimization model. Green across the board. Meanwhile, customers were complaining about inconsistent temperatures and rising energy bills. The monitoring was working perfectly; it just wasn't watching the right things.

Observability: The Mechanic's Diagnostic Computer

Observability is what happens when you take your car to a skilled mechanic. They plug in a diagnostic computer that can read hundreds of data streams from your car's systems. They can see the exact voltage from each sensor, the fuel mixture ratios, and the timing of spark plugs. More importantly, they can ask new questions on the fly: "Show me the oxygen sensor readings only when the engine is under load." For ML systems, observability means being able to answer questions you didn't know to ask in advance:

- "Their accuracy dropped 5%. Is this concentrated among users from a specific region or using a particular device?"
- "Prediction latency spiked. Is it correlated with the size of input data or one specific feature calculation?"
- "False positives increased. Can I see the distribution of all input features for just the incorrect predictions and compare them to the correct ones?"

The shift from monitoring to observability represents moving from watching for expected failures to being prepared for unexpected ones. It's the difference between having a checklist and having a detective's toolkit.

The Taxonomy of Failure: A Field Guide to Drift

During early consulting years, we saw every type of model failure imaginable. Through painful experience across multiple industries, we developed what we call the "Field Guide to Drift", a practical classification of how models fail in the wild.

Data Drift: When the Ground Shifts Beneath You

We experienced textbook data drift during the COVID-19 pandemic while working with a leading car rental company. The car rental demand forecasting model, which had been rock-solid for years, suddenly started making bizarre predictions.

The model considered factors like airport traffic, local events, and seasonal patterns; all the historical relationships we'd painstakingly learned. Then March 2020 happened. Airport rentals, normally the most predictable segment, vanished overnight. Local neighborhood rentals, which were treated as a minor segment, exploded. The statistical distributions of nearly every input feature had changed dramatically.

The Technical Reality: Data drift occurs when $P(X)$ changes; the distribution of your input features shifts, but the underlying relationship between features and target ($P(Y|X)$) remains valid. Your model's understanding is still correct; it's just being applied to the wrong context.

Detection Strategy: For numerical features, we had used statistical tests such as the Kolmogorov-Smirnov test. Here's the actual pattern we had implemented:

```
from scipy.stats import ks_2samp
import numpy as np
def check_feature_drift(training_data, production_data, feature_name, threshold=0.05):
    """
    Check if a feature's distribution has drifted significantly.
    This was part of our daily monitoring pipeline at Hertz.
    We ran this for our top 20 most important features.
    """
    statistic, p_value = ks_2samp(training_data, production_data)
    if p_value < threshold:
        print(
            f"Data drift detected in {feature_name}: "
            f"KS statistic: {statistic:.3f}, p-value: {p_value:.3f}"
        )
        return True
    return False
# Example from our rental duration feature
training_rental_days = np.random.normal(4.2, 2.1, 10000)  # Historical pattern
current_rental_days = np.random.normal(2.8, 1.5, 1000)  # Pandemic pattern
drift_detected = check_feature_drift(
    training_rental_days, current_rental_days,
    "rental_duration_days"
)
```

Listing 6.1: KS test for feature drift detection.

For categorical features, we used Chi-squared tests. The key lesson we learned: don't monitor every feature with equal intensity. Focus on your most important features; the ones with the highest feature importance scores from your model.

Concept Drift: When the Rules Change

The most insidious failure we've encountered was concept drift at a financial services client during the 2008 crisis. They had a credit risk model that had been performing beautifully for years. Then the financial world turned upside down.

```
import numpy as np
from scipy import stats
from scipy.spatial.distance import jensenshannon
import pandas as pd
class DataDriftDetector:
    """Monitor and detect data drift in production"""
    def __init__(self, reference_data: pd.DataFrame):
        self.reference_data = reference_data
        self.drift_threshold = 0.1  # JS divergence threshold
    def detect_drift(self, current_data: pd.DataFrame) -> dict:
        """Detect drift between reference and current data"""
        drift_report = {}
        for column in self.reference_data.columns:
            if self.reference_data[column].dtype in ['float64', 'int64']:
                # For numerical columns, use KS test
                stat, p_value = stats.ks_2samp(
                    self.reference_data[column].dropna(),
                    current_data[column].dropna()
                )
                drift_report[column] = {
                    'test': 'ks_test',
                    'statistic': stat,
                    'p_value': p_value,
                    'drift_detected': p_value < 0.05
                }
            else:
                # For categorical, use JS divergence
                ref_counts = self.reference_data[column].value_counts(normalize=True)
                curr_counts = current_data[column].value_counts(normalize=True)
                # Align distributions
                all_categories = set(ref_counts.index) | set(curr_counts.index)
                ref_dist = np.array([ref_counts.get(cat, 0) for cat in all_categories])
                curr_dist = np.array([curr_counts.get(cat, 0) for cat in all_categories])
                js_distance = jensenshannon(ref_dist, curr_dist)
                drift_report[column] = {
                    'test': 'js_divergence',
                    'distance': js_distance,
                    'drift_detected': js_distance > self.drift_threshold
                }
        return drift_report
    def generate_alert(self, drift_report: dict) -> bool:
        """Generate alert if significant drift is detected"""
        significant_drifts = [col for col, result in drift_report.items()
                              if result['drift_detected']]
        return len(significant_drifts) > 0
# We ran this weekly, once we had actual outcomes for predictions made 30-60 days prior.
# Get predictions from 30 days ago with now-known outcomes
def monitor_concept_drift():
    historical_predictions = get_predictions_from_date('30_days_ago')
    actual_outcomes = get_actual_outcomes(historical_predictions)
    current_accuracy = calculate_accuracy(historical_predictions, actual_outcomes)
    baseline_accuracy = 0.92  # Our established performance level
    if current_accuracy < baseline_accuracy - 0.05:  # 5% drop
        alert_team(
            "Potential concept drift detected",
            f"Accuracy dropped from {baseline_accuracy} to {current_accuracy}"
        )
```

Listing 6.2: Data drift detection class implementation.

Suddenly, the relationship between features (income, credit history, employment status) and the target (loan default) changed completely. People who would have been safe bets before were now defaulting. The model's fundamental assumptions about how the world worked were no longer valid.

- **The Technical Reality:** Concept drift occurs when $P(Y|X)$ changes; the relationship between your features and what you're trying to predict has shifted. Your model isn't just seeing different data; the meaning of the data has changed.

- **Detection Strategy:** This is much harder because you need ground truth labels. At the car rental company, a "delayed feedback" monitoring system was implemented:

The challenge we discovered is that ground truth often arrives weeks or months later. That's why we complemented this with business metric monitoring: if the model was failing, it should eventually show up in operational KPIs.

Prediction Drift: The Canary in the Coal Mine

At the same HVAC Manufacturing Company, we used prediction drift as an early warning system. We noticed that even before accuracy metrics began to degrade, the distribution of the model's predictions would often shift.

- **The Technical Reality:** Prediction drift occurs when $P(Y^{\wedge})$ changes; the distribution of your model's outputs shifts. It's a symptom rather than a root cause, but it's often the first signal that something is wrong.

- **Detection Strategy:** We implemented a simple but effective SQL-based monitor that ran hourly:

```
-- This query ran hourly in our data warehouse
- Monitoring prediction distribution for our churn model
WITH current_predictions AS (
SELECT
CASE
WHEN prediction_score > 0.7 THEN 'high_risk'
WHEN prediction_score > 0.3 THEN 'medium_risk'
ELSE 'low_risk'
END as risk_category,
COUNT (*) as count
FROM prediction_logs
WHERE prediction_time >= NOW() - INTERVAL "1 hour'
GROUP BY 1
) ,
baseline AS (
SELECT risk_category, expected_percentage
FROM prediction_baseline
SELECT
c.risk_category,
(c.count / SUM(c.count) OVER ()) * 100 as current_pct,
b. expected_percentage as baseline_pot,
ABS( (c.count / SUM(c.count) OVER ()) * 100 - b.expected_percentage) as difference
FROM current_predictions c
JOIN baseline b ON c. risk_category = b.risk_category
WHERE ABS((c.count / SUM(c.count) OVER ()) * 100_- b.expected_percentage) > 5.0;
- Alert if any category deviates by more than 5%
```

Listing 6.3: Hourly SQL query to monitor for prediction drift.

This simple monitor caught several issues before they impacted business metrics, including the time when a bug in the feature pipeline started sending default values for a key feature.

Building Your Proactive Warning System

After the HVAC predictive maintenance failure that started this chapter, we made a promise to the team: We would never again be blindsided by a model failure. We would build a warning system to detect problems before they reach customers.

This section details the practical system we built: a multi-layered defense that moves beyond simple thresholds to intelligent, adaptive monitoring.

Beyond Simple Thresholds

Using Statistical Process Control

Early in our careers, many of us made the classic mistake of setting static thresholds. "Alert if accuracy is 90%." This approach created two problems: false alarms during normal fluctuations and missed alerts when performance degraded gradually but significantly. For us, the breakthrough came when we learned about Statistical Process Control (SPC) from the manufacturing team. We used control charts to monitor production quality and realized the same principles applied to model monitoring.

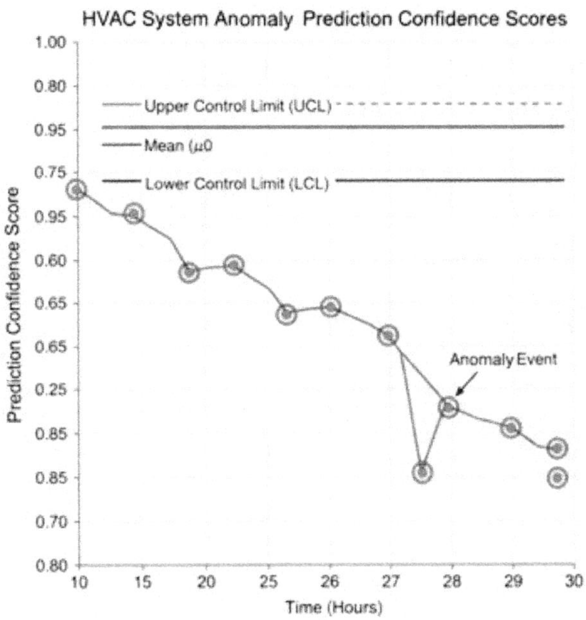

Figure 6.1. Statistical Process Control in action for model monitoring.

We implemented SPC for the key metrics:

- Instead of "alert if accuracy! 90%", we set "alert if accuracy drops 3 standard deviations below the 30-day moving average."
- Instead of "alert if latency > 100ms", we set "alert if latency shows 7 consecutive points above the mean."

This reduced the false positive rate by 70% while catching real issues earlier.

The Three Tiers of Metrics to Monitor

Through trial and error across multiple companies, we've developed a three-tier framework for ML monitoring. Each tier serves a different purpose and requires different tools and expertise.

Tier 1: System Health Metrics (Is the Engine Running?)

This is the foundation. If your model isn't running, nothing else matters. We learned this the hard way during our first on-call rotation.

- **Latency:** Track p50, p95, and p99 latencies. The p99 is crucial, as it tells you about your worst- case user experience.
- **Throughput:** Requests per second, but also track concurrency and queue lengths if you're using batch processing.
- **Error Rates:** HTTP status codes, but also business logic errors and model-specific errors.
- **Resource Usage:** CPU, memory, GPU utilization. We once caught a memory leak that would have taken down the service during peak hours.
- **Tools Use:** Prometheus for collection, Grafana for visualization, and PagerDuty for alerts.

The cloud-native solutions (CloudWatch, Azure Monitor) have improved significantly in recent months.

Tier 2: Data Quality Metrics (Is the Fuel Clean?)

This is where ML monitoring diverges from traditional software. Most model failures are data failures in disguise.

- **Data Drift:** We compute drift scores for the top 20 features daily using PSI (Population Stability Index) and K-S tests.

- **Data Quality:** Null rates, value ranges, categorical value distributions. We use Great Expectations to define and monitor data contracts.
- **Schema Validation:** Automatic detection of new columns, changed data types, or missing columns.
- **Feature Importance Stability:** We periodically retrain our model and check if feature importance rankings have changed significantly.
- **Real Example:** We detected that outdoor temperature readings from IoT sensors were suddenly showing values in Fahrenheit instead of Celsius. The data quality monitor caught the unit change before it affected predictions.

Tier 3: Model Performance Metrics (Is the Navigation Accurate?)

This is the hardest layer because it often requires ground truth, but it's the most important for business impact.

- **Online Performance: Capture** accuracy, precision, recall, and F1-score when the labels are available.
- **Business Metrics:** The ultimate measure of success. For the car rental recommendation engine, we tracked "conversion rate from recommendations" and "average rental value of recommended cars."
- **Proxy Metrics:** When ground truth is delayed, we use prediction confidence distributions, embedding clustering, or model uncertainty estimates.
- **Fairness Metrics:** Performance across different demographic groups, geographic regions, or customer segments.
- **Key Insight:** Don't wait for perfect ground truth. Even partial labels or business metrics can give you early warning of problems.

Data Observability: The Five Pillars

About five years ago, we started hearing the term "data observability" and initially dismissed it as a buzzword. Then we experienced a failure that changed our minds.

A pricing model at a car rental company that suddenly started making terrible recommendations. The tier 1 and 2 monitoring was green. It took two days to discover that an upstream data team had changed the calculation for "days until major holiday" without telling us. The feature still had the same name and data type, but the business logic had changed completely.

That's when we realized we needed what the industry now calls data observability: the ability to understand the health and state of data throughout its lifecycle.

1. **Freshness:** Is the data current? We monitor data pipeline execution times and SLAs. We used a daily pricing model based on competitors' prices. If that data was more than 4 hours old, we needed to know.

2. **Volume:** Is the right amount of data arriving? We track row counts for key tables. A 20% drop in daily transaction records was the first indicator of a processing issue.

3. **Schema:** Has the structure changed? We use schema registry patterns and validate against contracts. This would have caught the "silent failure" from Chapter 1.

4. **Quality:** Are the values valid? We check for nulls, ranges, patterns, and business logic violations. We validate that sensor readings are within physically possible ranges.

5. **Lineage:** Where did this data come from? We use data lineage tools to map dependencies. When a key feature started behaving strangely, lineage helped us trace it to a specific ETL job that had been modified.

Implementing these five pillars reduced the mean time to diagnose from days to hours. The tools have matured significantly, such as Monte Carlo, DataDog, and the open-source Great Expectations, all of which provide solid solutions.

In the Trenches and in the Boardroom

The technical implementation of monitoring is only half the battle. The other half, often more challenging, is organizational.

- How do you get teams to care about monitoring?
- How do you justify the investment to business leaders?

This section covers the human and business aspects of building your watchtower.

Field Story: The Silent Killer of a Fraud Model

While consulting for a mid-sized e-commerce company, we encountered one of the most subtle and dangerous failures we've ever seen.

The Setup: A Sea of Green Dashboards

Our team had built a sophisticated fraud detection model that had been running successfully for over a year. By all traditional monitoring standards, it was perfect. Latency was low, uptime was 99.99%, and the model's accuracy, calculated from manually reviewed transactions, remained stable at 99.5%. The dashboards were a comforting sea of green.

The Problem: The Finance Team's Spreadsheet

The first hint of trouble came from an unlikely source: the finance department's monthly loss report. Bottom-line fraud losses had been creeping up for three consecutive months. When the VP of Finance confronted the data science team, the response was defensive:" Their metrics are perfect. Your numbers must be wrong."

This created exactly the kind of organizational friction that kills data-driven cultures. Two teams, each armed with their own numbers, pointing fingers instead of solving problems.

The Investigation: Chasing Ghosts

The data science team launched a full investigation, but we were flying blind. Our monitoring dashboards showed nothing wrong. We re-validated the model on historical data, and it is still excellent. We checked for data drift on major features and found minimal changes. We verified that the prediction distributions were stable. After two weeks of fruitless investigation, frustration was mounting. The model, our pride and joy, was now viewed with suspicion by the business.

The Breakthrough: Asking a New Question

A group of architects joined the investigation and suggested stopping the search for answers to questions we already knew. Instead, we needed to ask new questions. We started exploring the data in ways that the predefined monitoring couldn't.

A junior data scientist had a hunch: "What if the problem isn't with their existing customers, but with new ones?" She started segmenting by payment method, and the results were startling:

```
# This analysis revealed the hidden pattern
def analyze_fraud_by_segment () :
# Segment by payment method
segments = df. groupby ('payment_method_type'). agg ({
'is fraud': ['mean'
, 'count'],
'prediction_score': 'mean'
})
# Found the smoking gun: BNPL (Buy Now Pay Later) payments
bnpl_data = df[df[ 'payment_method_type'] == 'BNPL']
other_data = df[df[ 'payment_method_type'] != 'BNPL']
print(f"BNPL fraud rate: {npl_datal'is_fraud' ].mean() :.3f}")
print (f"Other methods fraud rate: {other_datal'is_fraud']. mean():.3f}")
# BNPL fraud rate: 0.087 (8.7%)
# Other methods fraud rate: 0.009 (0.9%)
```

Listing 6.4: Analysis script to investigate fraud by customer segment.

The BNPL payment method, introduced six months earlier, had grown to 15% of transactions. Fraudsters had discovered that the model was blind to BNPL-specific patterns and were exploiting it heavily. Because BNPL was mixed with all other transactions, the overall metrics looked fine, while this segment was bleeding money.

The Aftermath

We immediately retrained the model with BNPL-specific features. More importantly, we implemented segment-aware monitoring that would track performance for each major payment method separately.

The lesson stuck with me: aggregated metrics can create a dangerous illusion of security. True observability means having the tools to discover problems you didn't know to look for.

The Business of MLOps: Quantifying the ROI

As you move into leadership roles, you will face a new challenge: justifying the significant investment required for proper monitoring and observability. Business leaders don't care about p-values or KS statistics; they care about ROI.

We had developed a framework for quantifying the value of MLOps investments across three dimensions:

Driving Revenue and Reducing Costs

This is the most direct way to demonstrate value. Every model should be tied to a business metric, and you should be able to calculate its impact.

Example from the Car Rental Company: Our car recommendation model showed a 4% click-through rate in A/B testing. The business value calculation looked like this:

Baseline: 2% CTR from previous system.

Improvement: 2 percentage point lift.

Scale: 10 million monthly impressions.

Value per Click: $0.75 (based on historical conversion data).

Monthly Value: 2% × 10,000,000 × $0.75 = $150,000.

When we could show executives that a model for monitoring investment would protect $150,000 in monthly revenue, the business case wrote itself.

Increasing Team Velocity

This is about measuring the efficiency gains from automation and better tooling.

Example from the HVAC Manufacturing Company: Before we implemented proper monitoring, diagnosing model issues took an average of 16 engineer-hours per incident. After implementing the observability platform, this dropped to 4 hours.

Time Saved: 12 hours per incident.

Incidents per Month: 3.

Hourly Rate: $75 (fully loaded cost).

Monthly Savings: 12 × 3 × $75 = $2,700.

More importantly, this freed up 36 engineering hours per month for innovation instead of firefighting.

Reducing Business Risk

This is the hardest to quantify but often the most valuable. It's about calculating the cost of failure.

Example from the Fraud Detection Story:

Fraud Losses Prevented: $50,000 monthly after fixing the BNPL issue.

Customer Trust: Harder to quantify, but we estimated $100,000 in potential customer lifetime value protected.

Reputation Damage: Even harder, but significant for a financial services company.

When we presented this as "Their monitoring investment of $X will prevent $Y in monthly fraud losses," the decision was easy for the business leaders.

We now use this simple template when proposing monitoring investments:

```
BUSINESS CASE: Model Monitoring Platform
1. PROBLEM
    - Current state: Manual monitoring, slow incident response
    - Impact: X hours/month spent on firefighting, Y$ in undetected model drift
2. PROPOSED SOLUTION
    - Automated monitoring platform with observability features
    - Cost: $Z per month
3. EXPECTED ROI
    - Revenue Protection: $A/month (from faster detection of model issues)
    - Efficiency Gains: $B/month (engineer time saved)
    - Risk Reduction: $C/month (prevented business losses)
4. PAYBACK PERIOD
    - Total investment: $T
    - Monthly benefit: $M
    - Payback period: T/M months_
```

Listing 6.5: A framework for creating a business case for an MLOps investment.

This framework has never failed us. When we can speak the language of business value, technical investments become much easier to justify.

Chapter Summary

Building an effective monitoring and observability practice is a journey that spans technical implementation, organizational change, and business alignment. The watchtower we've built together in this chapter has multiple layers:

The most important lesson we've learned across our careers is this: monitoring isn't a technical luxury; it's a business necessity. The companies that get it right treat their ML models not as one-time projects but as ongoing business operations that require constant care and feeding.

The 2 AM phone call we received about the failing HVAC model was embarrassing and costly. But it taught more about production ML than any textbook or course ever could. It forced us to move beyond academic metrics and pretty dashboards to build systems that protect business value.

In the next chapter, we'll explore how to take this foundation and scale it across the organization, building what we call the "ML Factory", a systematic approach to managing dozens or hundreds of models in production. Because as your watchtower grows from guarding a single model to protecting an entire portfolio, new challenges and opportunities emerge.

But for now, take these blueprints and start building. Your future self and future business leaders will thank you when the inevitable storms come, and your watchtower stands unwavering, helping you see through the fog and navigate to safety.

- **Foundation:** Understanding the different types of drift and failure modes through real-world stories from Hertz, Lennox, and consulting engagements.
- **Structure:** Implementing statistical process control and multi-tier monitoring with practical code examples.
- **Vision:** Embracing data observability across all five pillars with tools and techniques that work.
- **Impact:** Quantifying and communicating the business value with frameworks that resonate with executives.

CHAPTER 7

Advanced Deployment: From Black Boxes to the Physical World

In the last several chapters, we've built a robust factory for producing and deploying machine learning models into the cloud. But the world of ML is vast, and the standard request-response pattern is just the beginning. This chapter explores the frontiers of model deployment, moving beyond that standard pattern to tackle two major challenges.

First, we will journey into the "inner world" of the model's mind. We'll learn the practical, hands-on techniques of Explainable AI (XAI) to make their black boxes transparent and auditable. Then, we'll explore Human-in-the-Loop (HITL) frameworks, in which human experts and AI models collaborate to achieve results neither could achieve alone.

Second, we will explore the "outer world" of physical devices. We'll dive into the world of Edge Computing and TinyML, learning how to shrink powerful models to run on tiny, resource-constrained hardware, bringing intelligence out of the cloud and into the physical world.

Explainable AI (XAI)

A prediction, in itself, is a new piece of data. As data management leaders, our mission is to ensure the data assets the company relies on are trustworthy, auditable, and transparent. If the models are generating new, high-value data (predictions), we are responsible for ensuring that the data has a clear lineage and a comprehensible meaning. This is where Explainable AI (XAI) moves from a data science "nice-to-have" to a data governance "must-have."

Explainability is important for a data management initiative in:

- **Building Trust in Data Products:** Your primary job as a Data Architect is to build trust in your company's data. If a model is a "data product," its outputs must be trusted by the humans who consume them. A marketing manager is more likely to trust a churn prediction if they can see *why* a customer was flagged (e.g., "because their monthly usage dropped by 50%"). XAI is the bridge between a model's probabilistic output and human trust.

- **Debugging Data Pipelines:** This is one of the most underrated benefits of XAI from a data management perspective. Often, an explanation doesn't reveal a flaw in the model but rather in the upstream data. We once saw a fraud model in which the explanations for some strange predictions repeatedly highlighted the 'customer signup timestamp' as the most important feature. This made no sense. After digging in, we discovered a data-leakage problem in the ETL process: a bug was updating the timestamp every time a fraudulent event occurred, creating a perfect but spurious correlation. The XAI tool didn't just help to debug the model; it also served as a diagnostic tool for the entire data pipeline.

- **Compliance and Auditing:** This is a core data governance function. When an auditor asks why a particular automated decision was made, "the model did it" is not an acceptable answer. They need to see a complete trail. Data lineage shows the path of the data *to* the model. XAI provides the final link in the chain, showing the model's decision *logic*. For regulations like GDPR's "right to an explanation," XAI is not optional.

- **Fairness as a Data Quality Issue:** Model bias is often a symptom of underlying data quality issues. If historical data is biased, the model will amplify that bias. XAI tools are diagnostic instruments that help us detect the symptoms of this deep-rooted data quality problem, revealing whether a model is unfairly relying on features that may proxy for protected classes (like using 'zip code' as a proxy for race).

A Practical Deep Dive on Local Explanations

Local explanations are about understanding a single, specific prediction. They answer the question, "Why did *this specific customer* get this score?"

LIME (Local Interpretable Model-agnostic Explanations)

The core idea behind LIME is to approximate a complex black-box model with a simple, interpretable "imitation" model (e.g., a linear regression) in the immediate vicinity of a single prediction. Think of it as approximating a complex curve with a straight tangent line at a single point.

Data Management Use Case: Imagine a Master Data Management (MDM) system that uses a model to flag potential duplicate customer records. When the model flags a pair of records as a "potential duplicate" with 60% confidence, a data steward should review them. A LIME explanation can tell the steward *why* the model was uncertain (e.g., "the model was positively influenced by the similar names, but negatively influenced by the different addresses"), helping them make a faster, more informed decision.

SHAP (SHapley Additive exPlanations)

SHAP has become the industry standard for local explanations due to its strong theoretical foundations in game theory. It treats a model's prediction as a team's "payout" and fairly distributes credit for that payout among the "players" (the features).

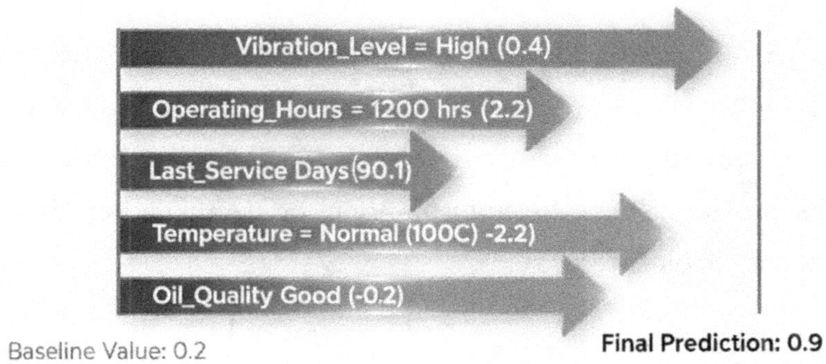

Figure 7.1. A SHAP force plot, providing a detailed, quantitative explanation for a single prediction.

Data Management Use Case: In a predictive maintenance model for factory equipment, a high failure prediction is generated for a specific machine. A SHAP "force plot" can be presented to the maintenance engineer. It might show that high 'vibration level' and 'operating hours' are contributing most to a high failure prediction, while a normal 'temperature' is pushing it back toward the safe range. This gives the engineer a specific, actionable diagnostic to check the machine's vibration dampers.

A Practical Deep Dive on Global Explanations

Global explanations help us understand the model's overall behavior.

Feature Importance

This tells us which features have the most predictive power *on average* across the entire dataset.

Data Management Use Case: When launching a new data governance initiative, a global feature importance plot is a powerful communication tool. You can go to the business and say, "Your three most important predictive models all rely heavily on customer demographic and product attribute data. This is why we must prioritize the data quality and stewardship of these specific data domains." It connects the abstract idea of governance to concrete business value.

Partial Dependence Plots (PDP)

A PDP shows how a model's prediction, on average, changes as a single feature's value changes.

Data Management Use Case: Imagine a data quality model that predicts the likelihood of a customer record being erroneous. A PDP can show the data stewardship team that, for example, "the model's predicted probability of error increases sharply if the 'last updated date' is more than 365 days old." This provides a data-driven justification for creating a new data quality rule or a process to regularly refresh older records.

Operationalizing XAI in a Data Management Framework

To be effective, explainability can't be an afterthought run in a notebook. It must be integrated into your MLOps pipeline and your governance framework.

1. **Explanation as a CI/CD Artifact:** Your CI pipeline should automatically generate a global feature importance plot and other key charts, embedding them in the Model Card for every new model candidate. This makes model review easier and more consistent.

2. **Explanation as a Service:** Your production model endpoint shouldn't just return a prediction. For auditable decisions, it could have an optional 'explain=true' parameter that also returns the SHAP values for that prediction in the API response.

3. **Storing Explanations for Auditing:** For every high-stakes decision (like a loan denial or a fraud block), your system should store the prediction, the unique ID of the model version that made it, and its corresponding SHAP values in a secure, immutable log store. This creates the complete, end-to-end audit trail that your compliance and governance teams require.

Human-in-the-Loop (HITL) Frameworks: AI-Human Collaboration

We have explored how to make the models more transparent. Now, we'll take the next logical step: designing systems where that transparency enables a powerful collaboration between the model and a human expert. This is the discipline of **Human-in-the-Loop (HITL)** systems.

A common misconception is that needing a human in the loop is a failure of automation. The reality is the exact opposite. A well-designed HITL system is a feature, not a bug. It is a mature architectural choice that acknowledges a fundamental truth: for many complex, high-stakes problems, the goal is not to *replace* human intelligence, but to *augment* it. It's about combining the speed, scale, and pattern-recognition of a machine with the domain expertise, contextual understanding, and ethical judgment of a human.

The Philosophy of HITL: Augmentation, Not Just Automation

Think of your model not as an autonomous employee, but as an incredibly fast and powerful co-pilot. The AI co-pilot can handle 99% of the routine flight checks, monitor thousands of sensor readings simultaneously, and flag potential anomalies that a human pilot might miss. But when it comes to making the final, critical decision in a complex, unforeseen situation like navigating a severe storm, the human captain is still in command, using the co-pilot's information to make a better, more informed judgment. A HITL system is designed with this philosophy. It automates the automatable and intelligently escalates the exceptions to the human expert.

Architectural Patterns for HITL

There are two primary architectural patterns for building HITL systems.

Pattern 1: Prediction with an Exception Queue

This is the most common and widely used pattern. The model handles the vast majority of "easy" or high-with cases automatically. Any case with low confidence, borderline status, or deemed high risk is automatically routed to a "review queue" for a human expert to make the final decision.

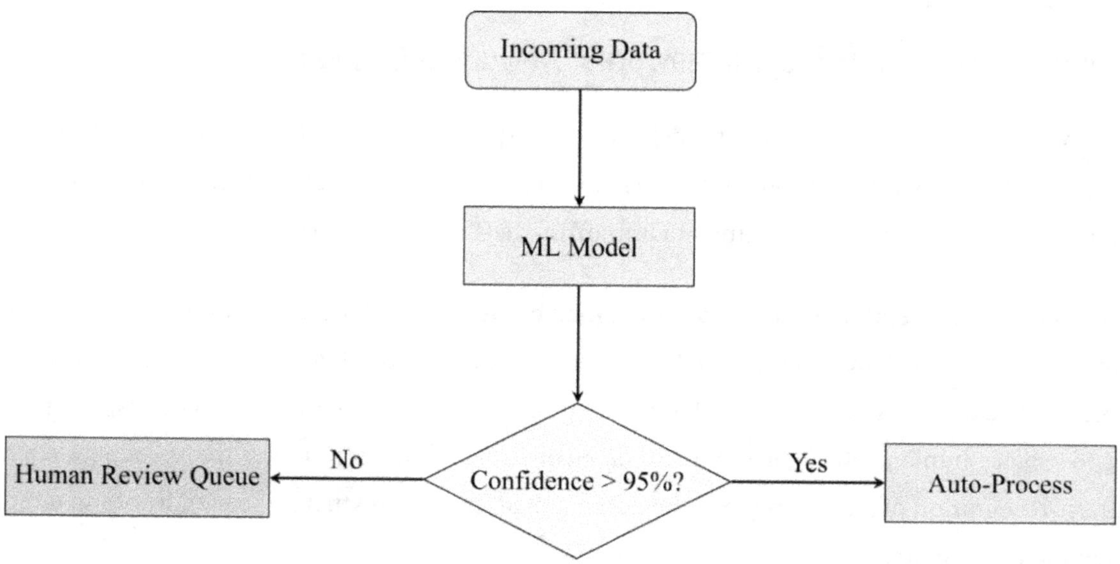

Figure 7.2. Flowchart for an Exception Queue with ML Model and Human Review.

Data Management Use Case: MDM Duplicate Resolution. In a Master Data Management (MDM) initiative, you often have millions of customer records that need to be de-duplicated. A machine learning model can be trained to predict the probability that two records represent the same person.

- If the model predicts a 99% probability that two records are a match, the system can **auto-merge** them.
- If the model predicts a 10% probability, the system can automatically mark them as **non-matches**.
- If the model is uncertain and predicts a 75% probability, it's too risky to automate. The pair of records is instead routed to a **data steward's review queue**. The UI can then present the steward with the two records side-by-side, along with a SHAP explanation for why the model was uncertain, allowing the human to make a fast, informed, and final decision.

This pattern dramatically increases the efficiency of the data stewardship team, allowing them to focus their valuable time on the most ambiguous and difficult cases.

Pattern 2: Active Learning

If the exception queue is about using humans to handle a model's failures, active learning is about using humans to make the model smarter over time. In this pattern, the model identifies the data points it is most *uncertain* about and proactively requests a label from a human expert. These new, high-value labels are then fed back into the system to retrain and improve the model.

- **The Analogy:** Active learning is like a curious student who knows what they don't know. Instead of re-reading the entire textbook, they ask the teacher specific, targeted questions to fill the biggest gaps in their knowledge. This is a much more efficient way to learn.
- **Data Management Use Case: Document Classification for Governance.** As part of a data governance initiative, a company needs to classify millions of unstructured documents (PDFs and Word docs) in its data lake as 'Contract', 'Invoice', 'Presentation', or 'Other'. A model is trained to do this automatically.

- The model classifies the 95% of documents it has high confidence in.
- When it encounters a new type of legal document, its confidence is very low.
- The active learning system flags this document and presents it to a legal expert in a simple UI, asking, "What type of document is this?"
- The expert provides the correct label. This newly labeled example is among the most valuable pieces of training data the model could receive, as it represents a genuine knowledge gap. This feedback loop continuously makes the model more robust and accurate over time.

Field Story: The Radiologist's Co-pilot

One of the most successful HITL systems was at a healthcare organization. They wanted to use AI to help radiologists read chest X-rays more efficiently. The radiologists' initial reaction was, understandably, one of skepticism and fear. They were worried that the company was trying to build a "robot radiologist" to replace them.

The project was on the verge of failure due to this human resistance before it even began. The data science team made a brilliant pivot. They reframed the entire project, not as an automation initiative, but as an **augmentation** initiative. They weren't building a robot; they were building a **radiologist's co-pilot**.

They designed a classic HITL exception queue system:

1. The AI model analyzed each X-ray as it arrived. The 80% of scans that the model predicted with very high confidence to be "clearly normal" were automatically tagged and moved to a lower-priority work queue.

2. The 20% of scans that the model flagged as potentially anomalous or was uncertain about were automatically prioritized and sent to the *top* of the human radiologist's work queue.

3. Crucially, when the radiologist opened one of these flagged scans, the AI's output was overlaid on the image, highlighting the specific area that it found suspicious (a form of explainability).

The impact was profound. The radiologists were not replaced; they were empowered. They could now clear the huge backlog of normal scans much faster and dedicate most of their expert attention to the most complex and potentially critical cases, using the AI's highlighting as a helpful starting point for their own diagnosis. The system was enthusiastically adopted because it respected radiologists' expertise and enabled them to work more effectively and efficiently. It succeeded because it was designed from the beginning as a human-computer collaboration, not an automation-at-all-costs solution.

Edge Computing and TinyML: Deploying Intelligence on Devices

So far, our entire discussion has been centered on the cloud. We've built models and pipelines assuming access to the virtually unlimited compute power, storage, and bandwidth of a massive data center. But the future of AI is not confined to these centralized brains. A new frontier has emerged, one where intelligence is pushed out of the data center and deployed directly onto the millions of devices that generate the data. This is the world of **Edge Computing** and **TinyML**.

This represents a profound paradigm shift. If cloud MLOps is like managing a fleet of massive, powerful cargo ships, then Edge MLOps is like managing a swarm of thousands of tiny, battery-powered drones. The core principles of MLOps still apply, but the constraints are entirely different, forcing us to rethink every part of the process.

The Paradigm Shift to the Edge: Beyond the Cloud

Why would you go to the trouble of running a model on a tiny, resource-constrained device instead of a powerful cloud server? The decision is driven by four key business and product requirements that the cloud simply cannot meet.

- **Latency:** For some applications, the time it takes to send data to the cloud, run a prediction, and get the result back is simply too long. An autonomous drone that detects and avoids an obstacle cannot wait 200 milliseconds for a round-trip to the cloud. It needs to decide in microseconds. Edge computing provides near-instantaneous inference by processing data at the edge where it is generated.

- **Privacy:** In an increasingly privacy-conscious world, sending sensitive data to the cloud is a significant liability. A smart home security camera that can distinguish between a family member and a stranger should not have to stream video of your living room to a corporate server. By running the computer vision model on the device itself, the raw data never leaves the home, providing a powerful, privacy-preserving architecture.

- **Bandwidth and Cost:** In many industrial or agricultural settings, internet connectivity is poor, intermittent, or expensive. A soil moisture sensor monitoring a remote farm field cannot stream high-resolution data to the cloud. By running a TinyML model on the device, it can analyze data locally and send only a tiny alert packet (e.g., "irrigation needed in sector 4") over a low-bandwidth network, saving high costs.

- **Offline Capability:** Some applications must function without an internet connection. A medical device in a rural clinic or a piece of industrial machinery in a factory basement must be able to make intelligent decisions reliably, whether it's connected to the internet or not.

The Art of Shrinking AI: Model Optimization Techniques

The primary challenge of the edge is the extreme hardware constraints. We are not talking about laptops or even smartphones, but tiny microcontrollers with less than 256 kilobytes of RAM, less memory than a single low-resolution JPEG image. Fitting a powerful neural network to such a device requires specialized optimization techniques.

Model Quantization

This is the most common and impactful technique. A standard neural network is trained using 32-bit floating-point numbers to represent its weights. Quantization is the process of converting these high-precision numbers into lower-precision integers, typically 8-bit integers (int8).

- **The Analogy:** This is like compressing a high-resolution, uncompressed WAV audio file into a much smaller MP3. You lose a tiny amount of imperceptible fidelity, but the file size is drastically reduced.

- **The Impact:** Since an int8 takes only one byte of memory compared to four bytes for a float32, quantizing your model's weights results in an immediate **4x reduction in model size**. Furthermore, many microcontrollers are highly optimized for integer math, meaning an int8 model can also run significantly faster and consume less power.

Model Pruning

Many large neural networks are over-parameterized; they have millions of weights, many of which contribute very little to the final prediction. Pruning is the process of identifying and permanently removing these unnecessary weights and connections from the network.

- **The Analogy:** This is like trimming a bonsai tree. You carefully remove unnecessary or redundant branches to reveal the tree's essential, most beautiful structure, making it lighter and more elegant without altering its fundamental nature.

- **The Process:** After a model is trained, a pruning algorithm identifies the weights with the smallest magnitudes (closest to zero) and sets them to zero. This creates a "sparse" model. The model is then briefly fine-tuned to allow the remaining weights to adjust and recover any lost accuracy. A carefully pruned model can be 50-90% smaller with a minimal drop in performance.

Knowledge Distillation

This is a more advanced technique that uses a large, powerful model to train a smaller one.

- **The Concept:** You start with a large, highly accurate "teacher" model that was trained in the cloud. You then create a much smaller "student" model with far fewer parameters. You train the student model not just on the raw data labels, but on the rich, probabilistic outputs of the teacher model. The student learns to mimic the teacher's nuanced, generalized behavior, achieving much higher accuracy than it would if trained only on hard labels.

The Edge MLOps Lifecycle

Managing a fleet of 1 million deployed edge devices presents unique MLOps challenges distinct from managing a handful of cloud servers.

- **Deployment:** You can't just 'kubectl apply' (create or update Kubernetes resources declaratively from files). Deploying a new model to devices in the field requires a robust **Over-the-Air (OTA)** update system. This system must securely push new model files to devices, verify the integrity of the update, and handle a potential rollback if the new model causes the device to crash.

- **Monitoring:** You do not have a real-time, persistent connection to your devices. Monitoring is often done in batches. A device might store its prediction logs and performance metrics locally and upload them only once a day when it connects to Wi-Fi. This means your monitoring data is delayed, and you need to build systems that can handle this asynchronous feedback.

- **Data Collection:** The devices are not just endpoints; they are also valuable data sources. Your MLOps pipeline needs a secure, efficient way to collect new, interesting data from the edge and feed it back into your cloud-based training loop. This is a critical part of the active learning and continuous improvement cycle.

Real-World Scenarios

- **Predictive Maintenance:** A TinyML model running on a $2 microcontroller is attached to an industrial motor on a factory floor. It continuously analyzes vibration patterns using an accelerometer. It runs for two years on a single coin-cell battery. 99.9% of the time, it does nothing but analyze the data on-device. But when it detects a specific vibrational frequency that signals an impending bearing failure, it uses a low-power radio to send a tiny alert packet to the factory's central control system.

- **Keyword Spotting:** The "Hey Siri" or "OK Google" function on your smartphone is a classic TinyML application. A tiny, power-efficient neural network is running on a specialized chip, always listening for just one or two specific phrases. The raw audio of your conversations never leaves the device. Only when that specific wake-word is detected does the device "wake up" and activate the larger, cloud-connected assistant to process your actual command.

Chapter Summary

This chapter has taken us beyond the standard cloud deployment. We have journeyed into the three frontiers of advanced MLOps, essential for building mature, responsible, and ubiquitous AI systems.

First, we unlocked the black box with **Explainable AI (XAI)**, transforming the models from opaque oracles into transparent, auditable partners. We learned practical techniques, such as SHAP and LIME, that are essential for building trust, enabling debugging, and meeting the rigorous demands of data governance.

Next, we embraced collaboration with **Human-in-the-Loop (HITL) frameworks**. We moved beyond a purely automated mindset to design systems in which the speed of AI augments human experts' judgment, leading to solutions that are more robust, efficient, and readily adopted in the real world.

Finally, we broke free from the data center with **Edge Computing and TinyML**. We learned the art of shrinking the models to run on tiny, resource-constrained devices, enabling a new class of applications that are faster, more private, and can operate anywhere in the physical world.

Together, these advanced patterns represent the next stage in the evolution of the deployed data scientist: building systems that are not just intelligent, but also understandable, collaborative, and truly present in the world around us.

CHAPTER 8

The Next Frontier: Building with Generative AI and LLMOps

This chapter marks a fundamental shift in our thinking. For the last seven chapters, we have focused on the discipline of deploying *predictive* AI. We've built models that act as brilliant critics, analyzing a dataset and predicting a number or a class. Is this transaction fraudulent? Will this customer churn? What will their sales be next quarter? These are all incredibly valuable but fundamentally analytical tasks.

We now turn to a new and profoundly different class of models: *generative* AI. These models are not critics; they are creators. They don't just analyze the world; they add to it, generating new, unstructured, and often surprising content like text, images, and code. This shift from prediction to creation is as significant as the shift from manual data analysis to machine learning itself.

As engineers and architects, you might feel the first instinct is to think the ground is moving beneath your feet, that the old rules no longer apply. The truth is the opposite. The discipline of MLOps, carefully built with the focus on data strategy, CI/CD, and monitoring, is not obsolete. It is more critical than ever. These powerful new models, with their unique failure modes and immense potential, demand an even greater level of engineering rigor. This new, adapted practice is what the industry is calling **LLMOps**.

The LLM Lifecycle: A New Set of Rules

The MLOps loop we know: data, train, deploy, monitor; still forms the backbone of the process. However, the nature of these steps is fundamentally altered.

From Feature Engineering to Prompt Engineering

In the world of predictive AI, we spend a lot of time on feature engineering. We are like master chefs, meticulously sourcing, cleaning, and preparing our ingredients (the data) before the cooking process can even begin. In large, pre-trained generative models, this focus shifts dramatically. The model is like a world-class improvisational actor who knows how to play a thousand different roles. Their job is no longer to prepare the ingredients, but to become a brilliant director. We must give the actor precise instructions to guide their performance. This new craft is called **Prompt Engineering**.

The meta-prompt on the facing page, which combines role-playing, detailed instructions, and a few-shot example, is a piece of code. A prompt is not just an input; it is a set of instructions, a persona, and a context that dictates the model's output. It is a form of "meta-modeling" where you are not training the model's weights, but rather guiding its vast, pre-trained knowledge base to solve your specific task. In an LLMOps world, prompts must be versioned, tested, and managed with the same rigor as their application code. Great AI output is not about the model, but it's about the prompt. Treat prompt writing as system design: roles, constraints, examples, and output format are your specification.

The Core Architectural Choice: Fine-Tuning vs. RAG

When building an LLM-powered application, you are faced with a crucial strategic decision. How do you imbue the model with the specialized, proprietary knowledge it needs to be useful for your business? There are two primary architectural patterns.

Fine-Tuning: Sending the Model to Medical School

Fine-tuning is the process of continuing the training of a massive, pre-trained model on a smaller, domain-specific dataset.

- **The Analogy:** This is like sending a brilliant, generalist doctor to medical school *again* to become a specialist cardiac surgeon. You are updating their core knowledge. They become true experts in that specific area.
- **Pros:** The model can achieve state-of-the-art performance on a very specific task. It can learn a unique style, tone, or proprietary vocabulary that is impossible to achieve with prompting alone.

Cons:

- **Expensive:** Fine-tuning requires a large, high-quality labeled dataset and significant GPU compute resources.
- **Stale:** The model's knowledge is now frozen because its training is incomplete. It knows nothing about events that happen after that date.
- **Opaque:** It can be very difficult to know *why* a fine-tuned model gave a specific answer, as its reasoning is baked into its millions of weights.
- **Catastrophic Forgetting:** The process of specializing can sometimes cause the model to "forget" some of its original, generalist capabilities.

Retrieval-Augmented Generation (RAG): Giving the Doctor a Library

This is the most popular modern architecture for building reliable, knowledge-intensive LLM applications. Instead of changing the model's brain, you give it access to an external knowledge base at the time of the query.

- **The Analogy:** This is like giving that same brilliant, generalist doctor a real-time, internet-connected library and a team of expert researchers. The doctor's core brain doesn't change. Still, they can answer questions about the very latest medical journals instantly by looking up the information first and then using their intelligence to synthesize an answer.

- **How it Works:** A user's query first triggers a search against a knowledge base (often a vector database). The most relevant documents are retrieved and passed to the LLM *as context,* along with the original question, in a single, large prompt.

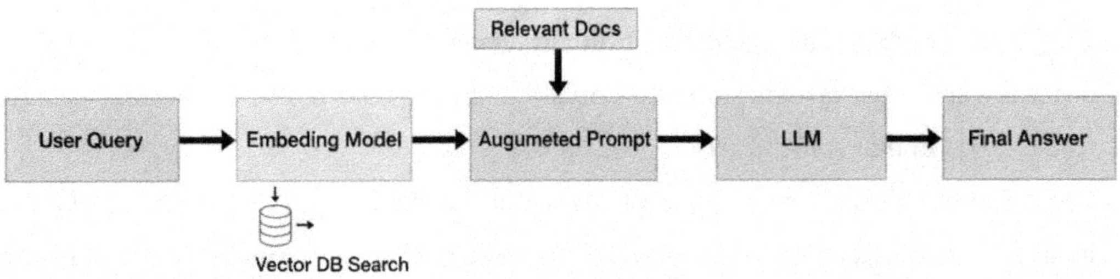

Figure 8.1. The architecture of a Retrieval-Augmented Generation (RAG) system.

The key components of a RAG system are:

- **Embeddings Model:** A model that converts text into a numerical vector, or "embedding." These vectors capture the semantic meaning of the text. Think of it as a Dewey Decimal System for concepts.

- **Vector Database:** A specialized database (like Pinecone, Weaviate, or Chroma) designed to store these embeddings and perform incredibly fast similarity searches to find the most relevant documents for a given query.

Pros:

- **Reduces Hallucinations:** The model is "grounded" in the provided documents, making it far less likely to make up facts.

- **Always Up to Date:** The model's knowledge is as up to date as the documents in your database. You can add, update, or remove information without ever retraining the model.

- **Auditable:** The model can cite its sources! Because you know exactly which documents were used to generate an answer, you have a clear audit trail.

When to Choose Which, and the Hybrid Approach

The choice between fine-tuning and RAG is a strategic one.

- **Choose Fine-Tuning when:** You need the model to learn a specific *style, tone, or skill.* For example, fine-tuning on your company's marketing copy to make the model write in your brand voice.

- **Choose RAG when:** You need the model to answer questions about specific, up-to-date, or proprietary *knowledge.* For example, building a chatbot that can answer questions about your company's internal HR policies.

In practice, many of the most powerful enterprise systems use a **hybrid approach**. They use a fine-tuned model to master a specific style and set of capabilities, and then use RAG at inference time to provide it with the dynamic, factual knowledge it needs to generate a relevant and accurate response.

LLMOps in Practice: Building the Guardrails

The shift from predictive to generative AI is exhilarating, but it also introduces a new class of risks. A predictive model that's wrong might produce a bad number. A generative model that's wrong can produce toxic content, leak private data, or confidently lie to your customers. The traditional MLOps playbook provides a solid foundation, but we need to build specialized guardrails for this new world.

This is the practical side of LLMOps. It's about adapting our CI/CD pipelines to test for things that aren't just right or wrong and implementing a new discipline of financial governance to manage the unique cost model of these powerful APIs.

CI/CD for LLM Applications: From Testing Answers to Judging Art

In the traditional MLOps pipeline, testing was a relatively straightforward affair. We could evaluate a predictive model against a set of ground-truth labels and obtain clear, objective scores for accuracy, precision, and recall.

Testing a generative model is more like judging an art competition. There is no single "correct" answer. Is the summary good? Is the tone on brand? Is the generated code efficient? These are subjective questions. Our CI/CD pipeline, therefore, needs to evolve from a simple test runner into a sophisticated evaluation platform.

```
class LLMCICDPipeline:
    """Continuous integration and deployment for LLM applications"""
    def __init__(self):
        self.test_suites = {
            'prompt_tests': [],
            'safety_tests': [],
            'performance_tests': [],
            'regression_tests': []
        }
    def run_prompt_tests(self, prompt_templates: list) -> dict:
        """Test prompt templates for consistency and quality"""
        results = {}
        for prompt in prompt_templates:
            test_result = {
                'format_validation': self._validate_prompt_format(prompt),
                'token_count': self._count_tokens(prompt),
                'safety_check': self._check_prompt_safety(prompt),
                'example_outputs': self._generate_example_outputs(prompt)
            }
            results[prompt.name] = test_result
        return results
```

```
def evaluate_model_outputs(self, test_cases: list, judge_model: str = "gpt-4") -> dict:
    """Use a more advanced LLM as a Judge to evaluate outputs"""
    evaluation_results = {}
    for test_case in test_cases:
        actual_output = self._generate_output(test_case['input'])
        judge_prompt = f"""
                Evaluate the following AI response based on these criteria:
                Input: {test_case['input']}
                Actual Output: {actual_output}
                Expected Criteria: {test_case['evaluation_criteria']}
                Please provide scores from 1-10 for:
                1. Relevance to the question
                2. Factual accuracy
                3. Completeness of information
                4. Clarity and coherence
                5. Safety and appropriateness
                Also provide brief justification for each score.
        """
        evaluation = self._call_llm(judge_prompt, judge_model)
        evaluation_results[test_case['name']] = self._parse_judge_scores(evaluation)
    return evaluation_results
def run_regression_tests(self, previous_version: str, current_version: str) -> dict:
    """Compare current version against previous to detect regressions"""
    regression_tests = self._load_regression_test_suite()
    regression_results = {}
    for test in regression_tests:
        old_output = self._get_historical_output(test, previous_version)
        new_output = self._generate_output(test['input'])
        similarity = self._calculate_semantic_similarity(old_output, new_output)
        regression_results[test['name']] = {
            'similarity_score': similarity,
            'significant_change': similarity < 0.7,  # Threshold
```

```
            'similarity_score': similarity,
            'significant_change': similarity < 0.7,  # Threshold
            'old_output': old_output,
            'new_output': new_output
        }
    return regression_results
def automated_safety_review(self, prompt: str, output: str) -> dict:
    """Comprehensive safety and content moderation check"""
    safety_checks = {
        'toxicity': self._check_toxicity(output),
        'bias_detection': self._detect_biases(output),
        'pii_leakage': self._check_pii_leakage(output),
    }
    return {
        'passed': all(safety_checks.values()),
        'detailed_results': safety_checks,
        'risk_level': self._calculate_overall_risk(safety_checks)
    }
```

Listing 8.1: A conceptual CI/CD pipeline for LLM applications.

This conceptual code illustrates the new test classes. We must build:

- **Prompt Testing:** Our prompts are code. A small change to a prompt can have a huge impact on the model's behavior. The CI pipeline must run a suite of tests on its prompt templates to detect regressions, unexpected changes in token counts, or newly introduced safety risks.
- **LLM-as-a-Judge Evaluation:** How do you automate the evaluation of subjective quality? The emerging best practice is to use a powerful, state-of-the-art LLM (like GPT-4 or Claude 3) as an impartial "judge." You feed the judge the original prompt, the model's response, and a rubric of evaluation criteria (e.g., "was the answer helpful?", "was the tone professional?"). This allows you to get a scalable, quantitative score for qualitative outputs.
- **Regression Testing:** When you change a prompt or fine-tune a model, how do you ensure you haven't accidentally made it worse on a task it used to do well? The pipeline should maintain a "golden dataset" of important prompts and their expected outputs. After every change, it runs these prompts through the new model and compares the new outputs to the old ones, flagging significant deviations.
- **Safety Review:** This is a non-negotiable gate. Every output from a candidate model must be run through an automated safety check that screens for toxicity, bias, PII leakage, and factual inconsistencies.

Cost Management and Governance: The Pay-per-Token Reality

In the world of predictive models, the highest operational cost was often the server running 24/7. It was a fixed, predictable cost. In the new world of LLMs, your highest operational cost is your model's *verbosity*. Most LLM APIs are priced per input and output token. This introduces a completely new, variable cost model that can spiral out of control without a new discipline of financial governance, or **FinOps for AI**.

A single user finding a loophole in your prompt that causes the model to generate a 10,000-word essay instead of a 100-word summary could cost you real money, very quickly. Your job as an architect is to build the systems that prevent this.

- **Real-time Tracking and Budgeting:** You must track every API call, count input and output tokens, and attribute the cost to a specific user, team, or feature. This allows you to set and enforce budgets and to fire alerts when you are approaching a limit.
- **Semantic Caching:** Many of the questions your users ask will be semantically identical. It is incredibly wasteful to repeatedly send the same question to an expensive LLM. A semantic cache stores the embeddings of previous questions. When a new question comes in, it first checks the cache. If a very similar question has been asked recently, it returns the cached response instead of making a new API call, saving both time and money.
- **Prompt Optimization:** The number of tokens in your prompt is a direct cost driver. An automated step in your CI pipeline can be to run your prompts through an "optimizer" that attempts to rephrase them to be more concise while maintaining the same quality of output.
- **Rate Limiting:** This is your primary defense against abuse. You must enforce strict limits on the number of calls a user can make per minute and the total number of tokens they can consume per hour or day.

In the age of generative AI, cost management is no longer just a finance problem; it is a core engineering and governance discipline that must be built directly into the applications.

Monitoring LLMs in Production: A New Breed of Metrics

We have now designed the guardrails for your LLM application's development and cost. The final, and perhaps most challenging, piece of the LLMOps puzzle is monitoring. In the world of predictive models, our monitoring watchtower was built on a foundation of statistical certainty. We could measure accuracy, precision, and recall against a known ground truth. With generative AI, that foundation of certainty turns to sand.

Why Traditional Metrics Fail

How do you measure the "accuracy" of a generated business strategy or the "precision" of a creative poem? The traditional metrics we relied on became nearly meaningless. Trying to apply them to a generative model is like judging a Shakespearean play with a spell-checker. The spell-checker can tell you if there are typos, but it can't tell you if the play is any good.

The failure of these old metrics became painfully apparent to us during one of the first major LLM deployments. We had built an internal chatbot to help our data analysts query the data catalog. The operational metrics were perfect: low latency, high availability, reasonable costs. But the user feedback was terrible. Analysts were frustrated because the model would occasionally invent plausible-sounding but completely fictional information. It would hallucinate table names or confidently misrepresent the contents of a data column. The traditional monitoring dashboards were a sea of green, while the users were losing trust in the system.

This experience taught us a critical lesson: to monitor a creator, you must become a critic. We needed to build a completely new monitoring dashboard, one designed to judge the quality of an essay, not just check the spelling.

The New Monitoring Dashboard

Monitoring an LLM requires a holistic approach that balances the quality of its output, the safety of its content, its operational performance, and its ultimate business impact.

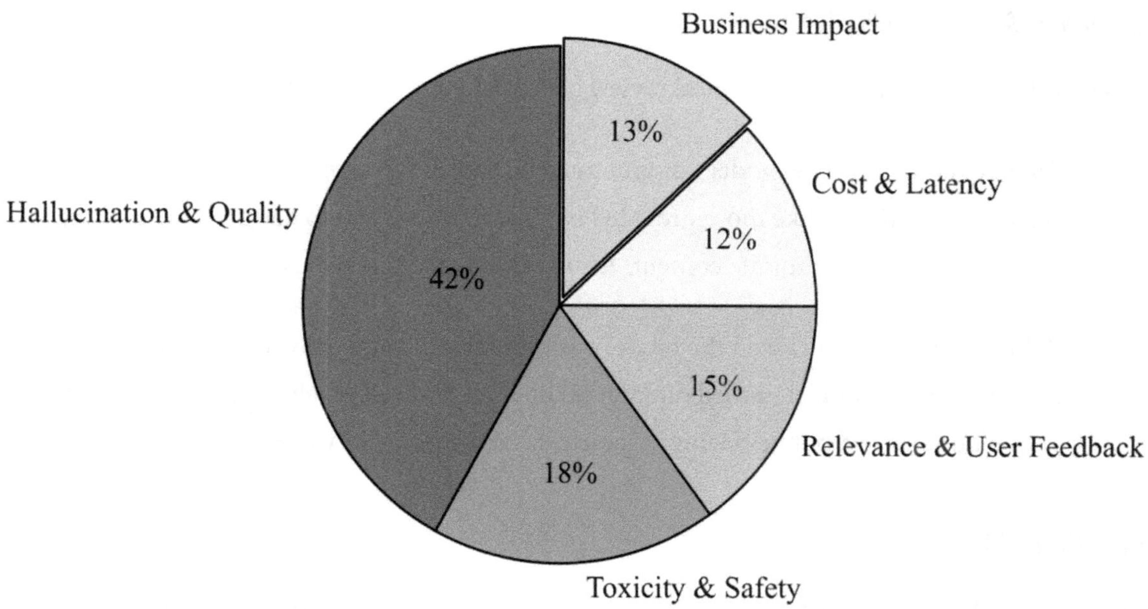

Figure 8.2. The LLM monitoring dashboard requires a new set of metrics.

The monitoring system, therefore, needs to be a multi-faceted critic, capable of tracking a new breed of metrics. Let's break down the key metrics this system tracks.

Performance and Quality Metrics

This is the core of your new dashboard, focused on the semantic quality of the generated content.

- **Hallucination Rate:** This is your number one quality metric. A hallucination is when the model generates factually incorrect or nonsensical information. In a RAG system, a common way to measure this is to compare the generated response against the source documents provided in the context, checking for contradictions. A rising hallucination rate is a critical alert.

- **Relevance and Coherence:** Is the model's answer relevant to the user's question? Is it grammatically correct and easy to understand? This is often measured using a combination of user feedback (a simple thumbs up/down button) and automated 'LLM-as-a-judge' evaluations.

Safety and Responsibility Metrics

These metrics act as an automated ethical review board for your model's output.

- **Toxicity and Bias:** The model's output must be passed through a safety filter or a separate classification model (like those provided by moderation APIs) to flag and measure the rate of harmful, biased, or unsafe content. A sudden spike in this rate is a P1 incident.
- **PII Leakage:** You must scan the model's output for any personally identifiable information. If a model trained on internal documents accidentally leaks an employee's phone number in a public- facing response, it's a major privacy breach.

Operational Metrics

These are the LLM-specific vital signs that track the cost and performance of your service.

- **Latency (Time to First Token):** For a streaming response, the most important user experience metric is not the total time to generate the full answer, but the 'Time to First Token'. How long does the user have to wait before the model starts "typing"? This is a key measure of your application's responsiveness.
- **Cost (Token Usage):** As we discussed, you *must* monitor the average number of input and output tokens per request. Tracking your token usage is essential for financial governance and preventing unexpected bills.
- **Embedding Drift:** This is the LLM-era version of data drift. In a RAG system, you are constantly converting incoming user queries into vector embeddings. You must monitor the distribution of these embeddings over time. A significant shift in this distribution can indicate that the semantic meaning of what your users are asking for has changed, which might require you to re-index your documents or update your prompt strategies.

Business Impact Metrics

This is the final and most important layer. It connects all the technical metrics to what the business cares about.

- **User Satisfaction:** Are users finding the answers helpful? This is often captured via a simple thumbs-up/down feedback mechanism.
- **Task Completion Rate:** If the LLM is designed to help a user complete a task (e.g., finding a document or writing an email), can it do so successfully?
- **Escalation Rate:** In a customer support chatbot, what percentage of conversations must be escalated to a human agent? A rising escalation rate is a clear sign that the model is failing to meet user needs.

Monitoring an LLM is a complex, multi-layered discipline. It requires us to become critics, safety officers, and financial auditors, all at once.

Field Story: Building an AI Co-pilot for Data Governance

The theory of LLMOps is one thing; putting it into practice under the pressure of a real business problem is another entirely. This is the story of how we built an AI co-pilot to solve one of the most persistent problems in data management: making the data catalog usable for everyone.

The Problem: The Data Catalog Black Box

We had done everything right, or so we thought. We invested in a sophisticated data governance platform, Alation, to serve as the central source of truth for the enterprise data. It was a beautiful library, meticulously organized and filled with valuable information. There was just one problem: we had built the library but forgotten to hire the librarians.

For the business users: the marketing analysts, the finance teams, the product managers, the data catalog had become a black box. The problem manifested in a thousand tiny moments of friction every day:

- A marketing analyst is spending an entire morning trying to figure out which of the five different tables named 'revenue' is the "right" one for the reporting.

- A finance team is using an outdated dataset for a critical forecast because they couldn't confidently verify its lineage.

- The data engineering team is being inundated with a constant stream of basic, repetitive questions: "What does the 'acct_stat_cd' column mean?"

- A senior leader made a strategic decision based on a metric he had fundamentally misunderstood.

The data was there, but the understanding wasn't. The catalog was a tool for experts, but it failed to empower the very people it was meant to serve.

The Solution: An Intelligent Data Guide

We envisioned an AI co-pilot that could act as that missing librarian. It needed to understand natural-language questions about the data and provide authoritative, context-aware answers grounded in their governance standards. The requirements were clear:

- Understand business questions ("Where do I find sales data?") and map them to technical assets ('fct_sales_daily').
- Provide trustworthy answers grounded in Alation's official documentation.
- Explain complex data lineage in simple, actionable terms.
- Scale to serve thousands of users across the global organization.

We built the system using an RAG architecture, indexing the entirety of the Alation metadata table schemas, column descriptions, business glossaries, user-generated comments, and lineage information into a vector database. The conceptual heart of our application looked like this:

```
class LLMCICDPipeline:
    """Continuous integration and deployment for LLM applications"""
    def __init__(self):
        self.test_suites = {
            'prompt_tests': [],
            'safety_tests': [],
            'performance_tests': [],
            'regression_tests': []
        }
    def run_prompt_tests(self, prompt_templates: list) -> dict:
        """Test prompt templates for consistency and quality"""
        results = {}
        for prompt in prompt_templates:
            test_result = {
                'format_validation': self._validate_prompt_format(prompt),
                'token_count': self._count_tokens(prompt),
                'safety_check': self._check_prompt_safety(prompt),
                'example_outputs': self._generate_example_outputs(prompt)
            }
            results[prompt.name] = test_result
        return results
    def evaluate_model_outputs(self, test_cases: list, judge_model: str = "gpt-4") -> dict:
        """Use a more advanced LLM as a Judge to evaluate outputs"""
        evaluation_results = {}
        for test_case in test_cases:
            actual_output = self._generate_output(test_case['input'])
            judge_prompt = f"""
                    Evaluate the following AI response based on these criteria:
                    Input: {test_case['input']}
                    Actual Output: {actual_output}
                    Expected Criteria: {test_case['evaluation_criteria']}
                    Please provide scores from 1-10 for:
                    1. Relevance to the question
                    2. Factual accuracy
                    3. Completeness of information
                    4. Clarity and coherence
                    5. Safety and appropriateness
                    Also provide brief justification for each score.
            """
            evaluation = self._call_llm(judge_prompt, judge_model)
            evaluation_results[test_case['name']] = self._parse_judge_scores(evaluation)
        return evaluation_results
    def run_regression_tests(self, previous_version: str, current_version: str) -> dict:
        """Compare current version against previous to detect regressions"""
        regression_tests = self._load_regression_test_suite()
        regression_results = {}
        for test in regression_tests:
            old_output = self._get_historical_output(test, previous_version)
            new_output = self._generate_output(test['input'])
            similarity = self._calculate_semantic_similarity(old_output, new_output)
            regression_results[test['name']] = {
                'similarity_score': similarity,
                'significant_change': similarity < 0.7,   # Threshold
```

Listing 8.2: Conceptual implementation of the data governance co-pilot.

The LLMOps Challenge: Taming the Creative Mind

The initial prototype was promising, but deploying it to a wider audience revealed the unique challenges of managing a generative model in a corporate environment.

- **The Hallucination Problem:** In an early test, a marketing analyst requested a table of quarterly revenue. The model, failing to find an exact match in its RAG context, confidently invented a plausible-sounding but completely fictional table named 'Q3 consolidated revenue'. The analyst nearly used this in a major presentation. This incident taught us that for an enterprise tool, a correct "I don't know" is infinitely better than a confident lie.

- **Tone Management:** The base model's conversational style was too casual. At one point, it responded to a complex lineage question with, "Whoa, that's a tricky one! Let's untangle this spaghetti code..." While amusing, this eroded the sense of authority we needed.

- **Cost Surprises:** Early usage patterns showed some users having long, meandering "conversations" with the system, asking dozens of follow-up questions. Because each turn of the conversation sent the entire history back to the API, these long sessions were generating unexpectedly high token counts and costs.

We had to build a new set of LLMOps guardrails to solve these problems, as shown conceptually below.

```
class GovernanceCopilotSolutions:
    """Solutions to real-world LLMOps challenges"""
    def solve_hallucination_problem(self) -> None:
        """Implement multiple layers of hallucination prevention"""
        solutions = {
            'strict_grounding': self._enforce_strict_grounding_in_prompt(),
            'confidence_thresholds': self._implement_confidence_thresholds(0.8),
            'source_verification': self._verify_all_citations(),
            'uncertainty_acknowledgement': self._train_model_to_say_i_dont_know(),
            'human_review_loop': self._implement_human_review_for_low_confidence()
        }
        return solutions
    def manage_tone_and_style(self) -> None:
        """Ensure professional, consistent communication style"""
        tone_management = {
            'style_fine_tuning': self._fine_tune_for_corporate_tone(),
            'prompt_constraints': self._add_tone_constraints_to_prompts(),
            'content_moderation': self._implement_real_time_content_moderation(),
            'user_feedback_loop': self._collect_and_incorporate_tone_feedback()
        }
        return tone_management
    def control_costs(self) -> None:
        """Implement comprehensive cost control measures"""
        cost_controls = {
            'semantic_caching': self._implement_aggressive_semantic_caching(),
            'query_complexity_limits': self._limit_complex_queries_per_user(),
            'response_length_management': self._optimize_response_lengths(),
            'usage_tiering': self._implement_usage_based_tiering(),
            'budget_alerts': self._set_up_real_time_budget_alerts()
        }
        return cost_controls
    def monitor_business_impact(self) -> dict:
        """Measure the actual business value delivered"""
        impact_metrics = {
            'reduced_escalations': self._measure_reduction_in_data_team_escalations(),
            'time_savings': self._calculate_average_time_saved_per_query(),
            'improved_decision_quality': self._survey_decision_makers(),
            'increased_data_catalog_adoption': self._track_catalog_usage_metrics(),
            'user_satisfaction': self._collect_user_satisfaction_scores()
        }
        return impact_metrics_
```

Listing 8.3: Solutions to LLMOps challenges in the governance co-pilot.

The Impact: Transforming a Data Culture

After implementing these guardrails, we rolled the co-pilot out to the entire organization. The results exceeded our expectations. We tracked a significant reduction in the time analysts spent finding the right data, and a 72% drop in the number of basic data questions escalated to the central data team.

But the most significant outcome wasn't measurable in a traditional ROI calculation: we had fundamentally changed the data culture. Business users who previously avoided the data catalog were now actively exploring and understanding data on our own. The AI co-pilot didn't just answer questions; it taught data literacy at scale. It finally fulfilled the original promise of the data catalog: to empower everyone to make better, data-driven decisions.

An Architect of Intelligence

This chapter has taken us to the current frontier of the field. We began this book by learning to think like architects of predictions: building robust, reliable systems that could forecast, classify, and recommend. As we stand at this new frontier of generative AI, our role is undergoing its most significant transformation yet. We are now becoming **architects of intelligence**.

This evolution doesn't render the MLOps expertise obsolete; it makes it more critical than ever. The principles we've mastered throughout this book: the discipline of reproducibility, the unwavering watchtower of monitoring, the guardrails of governance, and the engine of CI/CD form the essential foundation upon which reliable and responsible generative AI systems must be built. The new world of LLMOps is not a replacement for MLOps; it is an evolution built on top of it.

The rise of generative AI represents both an immense opportunity and a profound responsibility. As architects of these new intelligent systems, we're not just technical implementers. We're shapers of how our organizations think, decide, and create value. The systems we build today will become the cognitive infrastructure of tomorrow's enterprises.

The journey from a predictive critic to a generative creator is the most exciting frontier we've encountered, and the principles in this chapter provide your technical compass for navigating it. However, being a true architect of intelligence requires more than technical skill alone. It requires the strategic foresight to make durable, long-term decisions about the platforms, teams, and budgets that will power these systems.

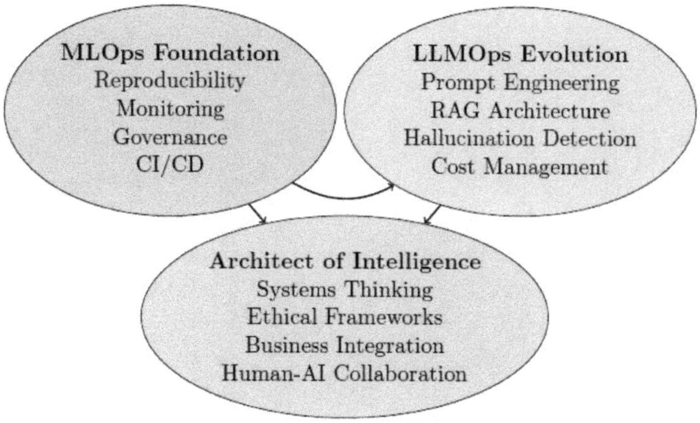

Figure 8.3. The evolution from MLOps practitioner to architect of intelligence.

Chapter Summary

Having mastered the engineering practices of the deployed data scientist, we are now ready for the final stage of the evolution. In the next chapter, we will step out of the engineering trenches and into the boardroom to explore the strategic playbook of the modern data leader.

- The focus of development shifts from feature engineering to Prompt Engineering as the primary lever for guiding a model's behavior.
- For enterprise applications, Retrieval-Augmented Generation (RAG) provides the most practical and reliable architecture for grounding LLMs in factual, up-to-date knowledge.
- The practice of LLMOps requires a new suite of monitoring metrics like hallucination rates and toxicity scores that go far beyond the statistical checks of traditional MLOps.
- With per-token pricing models, Cost Management and FinOps are no longer afterthoughts but first-class engineering and governance concerns.
- The role of the deployed data scientist evolves from an architect of predictions to an architect of intelligence, responsible for building collaborative, human-AI systems.

Chapter Summary

CHAPTER 9

Data Leader's Playbook: Navigating the New Frontier

For the last eight chapters, we have been on a journey together, deep in the engineering trenches. We've learned the MLOps discipline required to build, deploy, and manage production-grade data products. We've gone from a single developer to an architect.

But in this final chapter, we must evolve one more time. We are going to climb out of the trenches and step into the boardroom. Our task is no longer to build the data product; it's to build the *organization* that builds the data products. This chapter is the leader's playbook. It's about navigating the complex, high-stakes, and rapidly changing landscape of technology, vendors, budgets, and people. Your success as a data leader will not be measured by the elegance of your code, but by your ability to make the right strategic decisions that empower your entire organization to create value from data.

The FAANG Fallacy: Why You Can't 'Throw Money at the Problem'

The first challenge a new data leader faces is the immense pressure from the business to "be more like Google." Executives read about the legendary data platforms at Netflix, Meta, or Amazon and ask a simple question: "Why can't they just build that here?" You would have seen this movie play out so many times. A company will hire a team of expensive ex-FAANG engineers and give them a hundred-million-dollar budget to build their own internal, custom-built data platform from scratch. Two years later, the budget is gone, the team is burned out, and the business has nothing to show for it but a few half- finished, experimental tools. This approach is a trap. It's based on a fundamental misunderstanding of what those FAANG platforms are. They weren't born from some elegant, top-down grand plan. They were, in large part, **historical accidents**. They were glorious, complex, and incredibly expensive kludges built over decades out of sheer necessity. When these companies were solving petabyte-scale problems, the cloud didn't exist. Managed data warehouses, open-source Spark, and Kafka were not available. They had no choice but to build everything themselves, from custom file systems to their own workflow schedulers. They could do this for two reasons:

1. They had a technology-first, not a core-business-first, strategy.
2. They had tens of thousands of platform engineers and budgets in the hundreds of millions to "throw money at the problem".

As an enterprise in retail, manufacturing, or banking, you cannot, and *should not*, try to replicate this path. Your job is not to build a world-class query engine; it's to sell products, manage risk, or build products. The central challenge for us, the "un-fanged" organizations, is this: they **need** FAANG-like outcomes (scale, reliability, self-service), but they cannot replicate the FAANG-level cost or resource model.

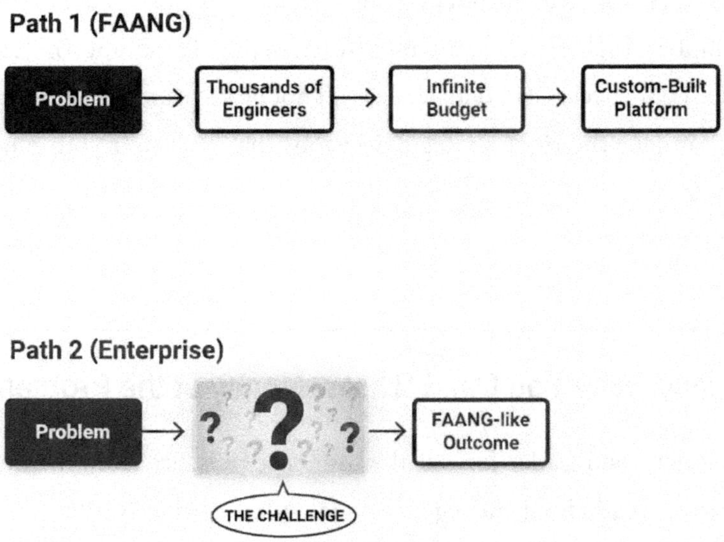

Figure 9.1. The FAANG Fallacy: Un-fanged organizations need the same outcomes but cannot follow the same path.

The Architect's Choice: Buy the Infrastructure, Build the Advantage

The solution to this dilemma is not a simple "build vs. buy" choice. The answer is a hybrid: **Buy the infrastructure, but build the design patterns.** This is the sensible middle path.

In 2026, it is engineering malpractice to build your own data warehouse engine, streaming platform, or ingestion tool from scratch. The open-source and SaaS ecosystems have commercialized the FAANG's struggles, giving us incredible off-the-shelf power. We "buy" (or adopt) the powerful, managed, and scalable foundation:

- **The Data Platform:** A cloud data Lakehouse like Snowflake or Databricks.
- **The Ingestion Layer:** A managed tool like Fivetran or Airbyte.
- **The Open Standards:** We should insist on open table formats like **Apache Iceberg** and open file formats like **Apache Parquet**.

This managed foundation delivers FAANG-like scale and reliability at a fraction of the cost.

This is where we must focus our precious, finite engineering resources. We don't get a competitive advantage from building a better query engine. We get an advantage by applying our unique business knowledge *on top* of that engine. We "build" the business-specific design patterns that make the platform useful for the company:

- **The Semantic Models:** The specific dbt models that define 'customer', 'revenue', and 'churn' for the business.
- **The Data Contracts:** The governance-as-code frameworks that enforce the data quality rules.
- **The Data Products:** The specific, versioned, and monitored models and APIs that solve the business problems.

This hybrid approach lets us inherit a scalable foundation and focus our engineering on what matters: our unique business logic.

The Internal Data Platform: A "Data Ecosystem" for Your Enterprise

This hybrid model has a name: the **Internal Data Platform (IDP)**, or the "Data Developer Platform" (DDP). This is the real secret of FAANG. Their advantage wasn't just their tools; it was that they built better systems of *abstraction*. They built internal, self-service platforms that abstracted away the infrastructure complexity, allowing their data scientists to act with incredible leverage. As a data leader, your goal is to build this "Data Ecosystem" for your enterprise. Your job is no longer to be the gatekeeper of a central pipeline. Your job is to be an enabler. You build the "paved road" that empowers your domain teams to build their own data products safely and efficiently. This platform is the technical embodiment of the "Data-First" philosophy discussed in Chapter 2. Instead of a brittle, pipeline-first approach where a single failure cascades to everything downstream, we build a system where data itself serves as the decoupling layer. The transformation pipelines don't fail if the ingestion is late; they wait for the fresh data to be ready, then they run. This separation of concerns, built on a platform, is what creates a resilient and scalable data culture.

Navigating the Great Consolidation: Enclosure vs. Unification

Just as we've settled on this new, hybrid model, the ground shifts again. The golden age of modular, best-of-breed tools is ending. A wave of consolidation is upon us. Vendors are racing to acquire their way across the stack: ingestion, acquisition, transformation, observability, monitoring, analytics, and collaboration. They are all selling the same story: **unification**. As a data leader, your most important job right now is to see through the marketing. You must learn to distinguish between:

- **Narrative Unification (The Marketing Story):** This is a **bolt-on acquisition**. It's a collection of different tools stitched together, all flying under one logo and one contract. Under the hood, the metadata layers don't talk to each other, the security models are different, and the workflows are disjointed. This is not unification; it's **enclosure**. It's a defensive moat designed to increase switching costs and lock you into their ecosystem.

- **Architectural Unification (The Engineering Truth):** This is the real prize. It's a platform built on a **single, shared substrate** for metadata, security, and semantics. The layers don't just sit side by side; they share the same governance model and operational backbone. This is rare, but it's what they must demand.

How to Avoid the Trap

When a vendor pitches you a "unified, end-to-end platform," you must be the skeptical architect.

- **Ask the Hard Questions:** "Was this feature built in-house, or was it an acquisition? If so, does it share the same IAM model, or do I have to manage permissions in two places?"
- **Insist on Open Standards:** True unification lowers switching costs by aligning with open standards; enclosure raises them. Is your platform built on open formats like Iceberg, Delta, and Parquet? Or is your data trapped in a proprietary format?
- **Calculate the Exit Cost:** The risk of false unification is not just vendor lock-in; it's the misallocation of your budget and years of engineering time to a platform that delivers only fragmentation and higher switching costs.

Building and Scaling Data and AI Teams

Making the right architectural decisions is only half the battle. A brilliant platform with the wrong team structure will fail just as surely as a brilliant team with the wrong platform. As a data leader, your second job, after setting the technical strategy, is to build the human organization to execute it.

In the early days, the title "Data Scientist" was a catch-all for anyone who could write SQL, build a model, and make a chart. The modern data organization, however, requires a team of specialists.

- **The Data Scientist (The 'Why'):** The core researcher and innovator. Their job is to explore the data, formulate hypotheses, and build the initial models to solve business problems.

- **The Machine Learning Engineer (The 'How'):** The bridge from the lab to production. They are software engineers who specialize in MLOps, responsible for building robust, scalable, and automated systems to deploy, monitor, and maintain models.

- **The Analytics Engineer (The 'What'):** This is a newer, critical role. The Analytics Engineer uses tools like dbt to transform raw data into the clean, reliable, and well-documented "gold" layer data models that the entire business runs on.

- **The Data Product Manager (The 'Who' and 'For What'):** The Data PM is responsible for the vision, strategy, and roadmap of the data products, ensuring that what the team builds drives business value.

How you organize these specialists is a critical leadership decision.

- **Centralized (Center of Excellence):** All data professionals are part of a single, central team. This is great for starting out and setting standards, but it can quickly become a bottleneck.

- **Embedded (Decentralized):** Data professionals are hired directly into the business units (e.g., Marketing, Finance). This ensures deep business alignment but can lead to a chaotic proliferation of tools and standards.

- **Hybrid (The Modern Choice):** This is the model that most mature data organizations converge on. A central **Platform Team** (as discussed in their DDP model) builds and maintains the shared infrastructure, tools, and governance frameworks. Data Scientists and Analytics Engineers are then **embedded** within the business units, using the central platform to build their specific data products. This structure provides both centralized leverage and decentralized, business-aligned execution.

The Economics of AI: Managing the FinOps Frontier

As a data leader, you are not just a technologist; you are a business owner. And every business owner must manage their budget. The cloud offers incredible power, but with that power comes the risk of an equally incredible bill. A core part of your job is to build a culture of financial accountability and to master the discipline of **FinOps** (Financial Operations).

Three primary components drive your monthly cloud bill:

1. **Compute:** The cost of the virtual machines and containers that run your model training jobs and production inference services.
2. **Storage:** The cost of storing your data in the data lake (S3, GCS) and the data warehouse (Snowflake, BigQuery).
3. **Data Egress:** The "hidden" cost. Cloud providers do not charge for data entering their networks, but they charge a significant fee for every gigabyte of data leaving their *networks.*

Practical Cloud Optimization Strategies

- **Embrace Spot Instances for Training:** Model training jobs are often fault-tolerant, making them perfect for Spot Instances, which offer discounts of up to 90%.
- **Right-Size Your Servers:** Use your monitoring dashboards (Chapter 6) to track the resource utilization of your production services and continuously "right-size" them to the smallest instance type that can comfortably handle the load.
- **Implement Data Lifecycle Policies:** Automatically move older, less frequently accessed data to lower-cost, archival storage tiers such as **Amazon S3 Glacier**.
- **Shut Down Idle Resources:** Implement automated scripts to shut down non-production development and staging environments overnight and on weekends.

Chapter Summary

This brings us to the end of our journey. We started as developers, learning to think like data scientists. We evolved into architects, learning to build robust, production-ready systems. This final chapter is about the last, and most important, evolution: from an architect to a data statesperson. A statesperson is a leader who can navigate the complex political and economic landscape to make wise, long-term decisions. The data landscape is now a political and economic one, dominated by vendors vying for control. Your final and most critical job as a data leader is to see through the narratives, to understand the architectural truths, and to build a data strategy: of platforms, people, and processes that serve your business's long-term interests, not just a vendor's bottom line.

- Do not try to replicate FAANG's architectures; they were historical accidents built with massive resources. Instead, focus on replicating their *outcomes.*
- The best strategy for most companies is a hybrid one: **Buy the infrastructure but build the design patterns** that represent your unique business logic.
- Your goal as a leader is to build an **Internal Data Platform (IDP)** that provides abstractions and self-service capabilities, enabling a resilient "data-first" culture.
- Be wary of vendor consolidation. Learn to distinguish **narrative unification** (marketing) from **architectural unification** (a shared substrate).
- Insist on **open standards** like Iceberg and Parquet to avoid vendor lock-in and calculate the total cost of exit, not just the cost of entry.
- Structure your teams using a **hybrid model,** with a central platform team enabling embedded, business-facing data experts.
- Master the **Economics of AI** (FinOps) by optimizing compute, storage, and egress, and by justifying all investments in terms of business ROI.

Bibliography

Michael Armbrust, Ali Ghodsi, Reynold Xin, and Matei Zaharia. Lakehouse: A new generation of open platforms that unify data warehousing and advanced analytics. *CIDR*, 2021. URL https://www.cidrdb.org/cidr2021/papers/cidr2021 paper17.pdf.

Google Cloud. Generative AI at Google. https://cloud.google.com/ai/generative-ai, 2023. Accessed: 2025-01-15.

Ralph Kimball and Margy Ross. *The data warehouse toolkit: The definitive guide to dimensional modeling*. John Wiley & Sons, 2013.

Patrick Lewis, Ethan Perez, Aleksandra Piktus, Fabio Petroni, Vladimir Karpukhin, Naman Goyal, Heinrich Küttler, Mike Lewis, Wen-tau Yih, Tim Rocktäschel, et al. Retrieval-augmented generation for knowledge-intensive NLP tasks. *Advances in Neural Information Processing Systems*, 33: 9459–9474, 2020. URL https://arxiv.org/abs/2005.11401.

Scott M Lundberg and Su-In Lee. A unified approach to interpreting model predictions. In *Advances in neural information processing systems*, pages 4765–4774, 2017. URL https://arxiv.org/abs/1705.07874. The original SHAP paper.

Margaret Mitchell, Simone Wu, Andrew Zaldivar, Parker Barnes, Lucy Vasserman, Ben Hutchinson, Elena Spitzer, Inioluwa Deborah Raji, and Timnit Gebru. Model cards for model reporting. In *Proceedings of the conference on fairness, accountability, and transparency*, pages 220–229, 2019. URL https://arxiv.org/abs/1810.03993.

Marco Tulio Ribeiro, Sameer Singh, and Carlos Guestrin. " Why should I trust you?" Explaining the predictions of any classifier. In *Proceedings of the 22nd ACM SIGKDD international conference on knowledge discovery and data mining*, pages 1135–1144, 2016. URL https://arxiv.org/abs/1602.04938. The original LIME paper.

Stefan Studer, Thanh Binh Bui, Christian Drescher, Alexander Hanuschkin, Ludwig Winkler, Steven Peters, and Klaus-Robert Müller. Towards crisp-ml(q): A machine learning process model with quality assurance methodology. *Machine Learning and Knowledge Extraction*, 3(2):392–413, 2021. URL https://doi.org/10.3390/make3020020.

Pete Warden and Daniel Situnayake. *TinyML: Machine learning with TensorFlow Lite on Arduino and ultra-low-power microcontrollers*. O'Reilly Media, 2019.

Index

www.ingramcontent.com/pod-product-compliance
Lightning Source LLC
LaVergne TN
LVHW060035210926
848481LV00013B/3871